P9-CQZ-504

Grade 2

KUMON WRITING WORKBOOKS

Writing

Table of Contents

KUMON

Date 4/13/21   Name Gabriel

1 Trace each word. Then read it aloud.

3 points each

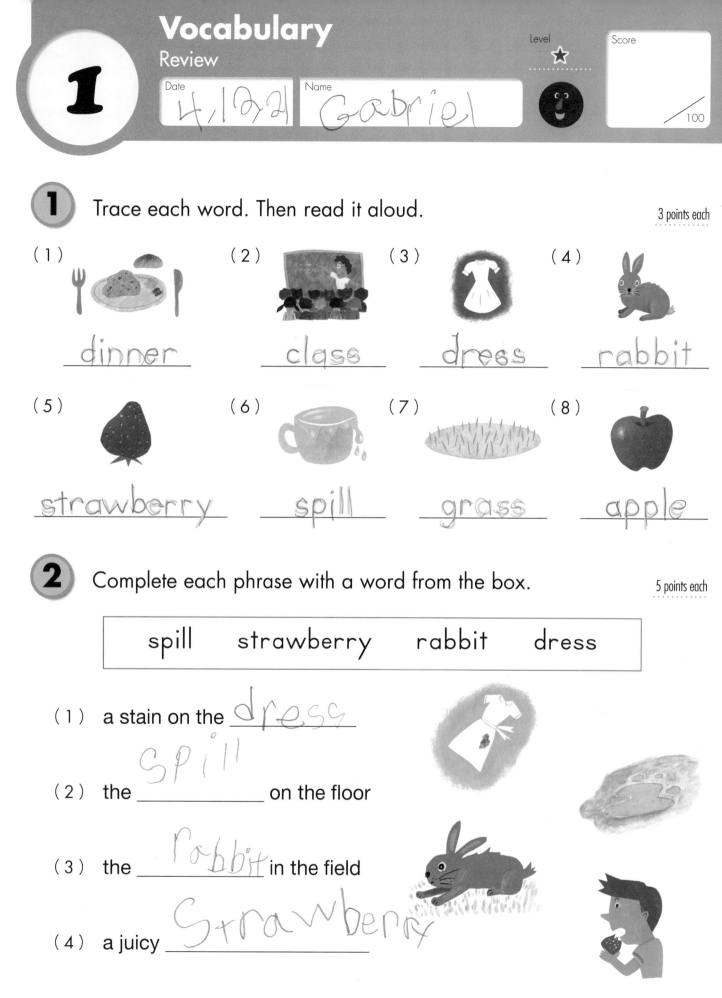

(1) dinner

(2) class

(3) dress

(4) rabbit

(5) strawberry

(6) spill

(7) grass

(8) apple

2 Complete each phrase with a word from the box.

5 points each

spill	strawberry	rabbit	dress

(1) a stain on the _dress_

(2) the _spill_ on the floor

(3) the _rabbit_ in the field

(4) a juicy _strawberry_

3 Write the word that matches each picture.

4 points each

(1) dinner

(2) clagg

(3) strawberr

(4) grgss

(5) Apple

4 Complete each sentence with a word from the box.

6 points each

| spill | dinner | class | grass | dress | rabbit |

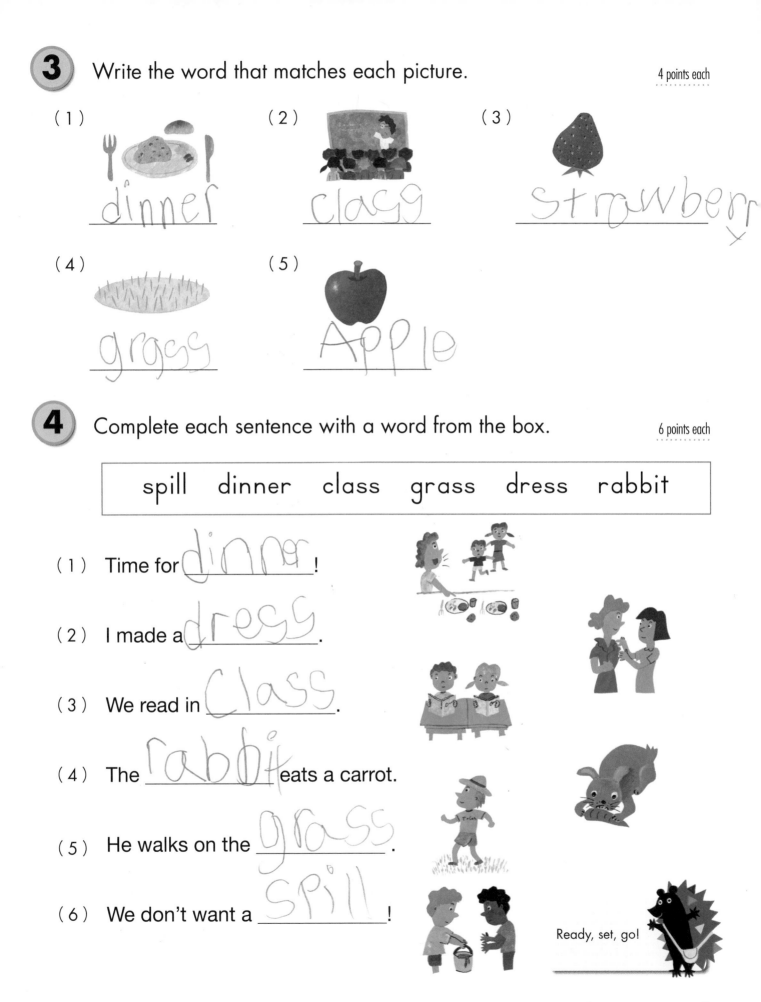

(1) Time for dinnr !

(2) I made a dregg .

(3) We read in Class .

(4) The rabbit eats a carrot.

(5) He walks on the grass .

(6) We don't want a Spill !

Ready, set, go!

Long Vowel Sounds
Review

2

Level ☆

Score

Date 4/14/2024 Name Gabriel

100 /100

1 Trace the missing vowel or vowels and read the word aloud. Then match each word to its picture.

3 points each

(1) bay

(2) train

(3) sea

(4) sheep

(5) hike

(6) slide

(7) rope

(8) bone

(9) blue

(10) flute

ⓐ ⓑ ⓒ ⓓ ⓔ ⓕ ⓖ ⓗ ⓘ ⓙ

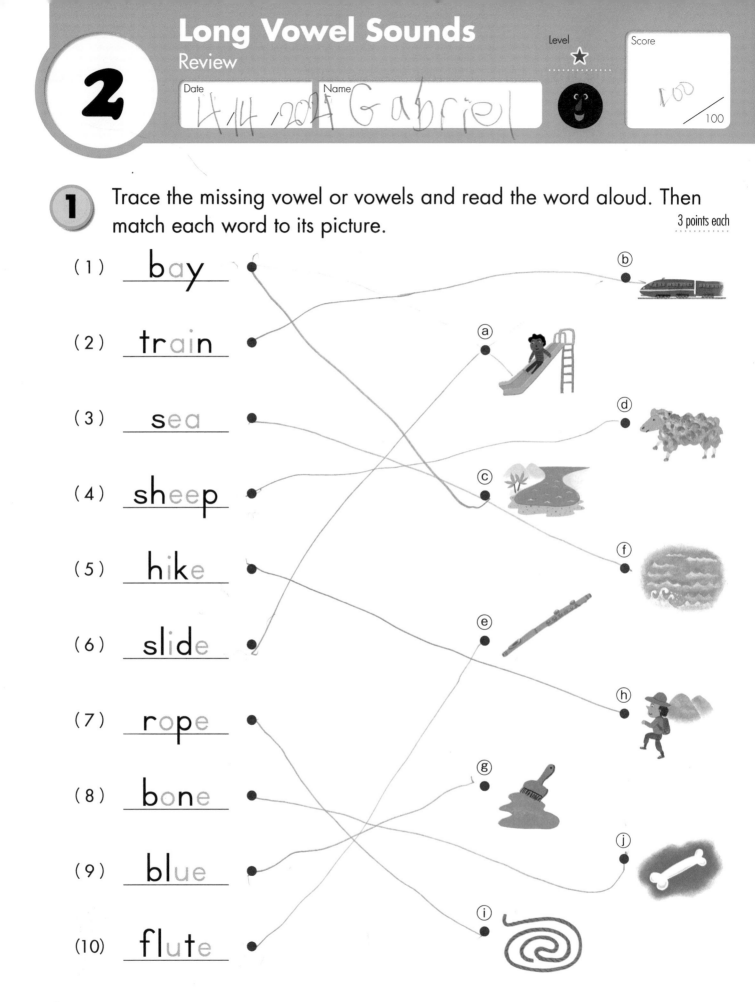

2 Write the rhyming word to complete the rhyming pair.

5 points each

(1) glue _blue_

(2) brain _train_

(3) hay _bay_

(4) flea _sea_

(5) bike _hike_

(6) sleep _sheep_

(7) ride _slide_

(8) phone _bone_

3 Complete each phrase with a word from the box.

5 points each

slide   flute   rope   bone   phone   sleep

(1) a toad plays the _flute_

(2) pull the boat by a _rope_

(3) hide by the _slide_

(4) a _bone_ in a hole

(5) _sleep_ on the train

(6) hear a tune on the _phone_

Good job!

Vocabulary

Date 4 ,2621   Name Gabriel

Level ☆

Score   /100

1 Trace each word. Then read it aloud.

3 points each

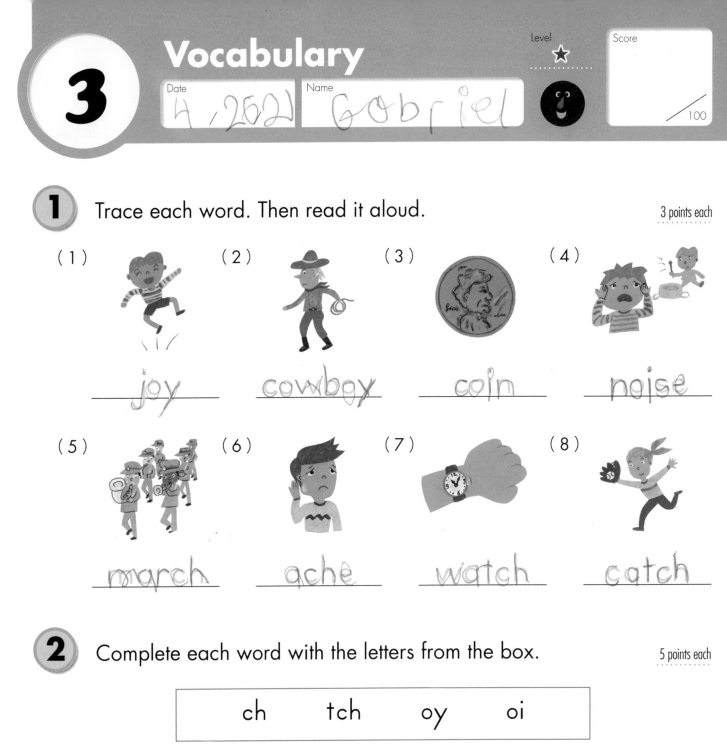

(1) joy

(2) cowboy

(3) coin

(4) noise

(5) march

(6) ache

(7) watch

(8) catch

2 Complete each word with the letters from the box.

5 points each

| ch | tch | oy | oi |

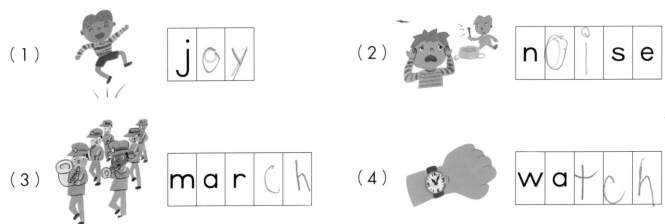

(1) j o y

(2) n o i s e

(3) m a r c h

(4) w a t c h

3 Trace the missing letters. Then write the missing word. 4 points each

(1)

destroy   cowboy

(2)

point   coin

(3)

chicken   march

(4)

scratch   catch
scratch

(5)

anchor   ache

4 Complete each sentence with a word from the box. 6 points each

anchor	destroy	point	scratch	chicken	march

(1) The cat wanted to ___scratch___ me.

(2) I watch the band ___march___.

(3) The ___point___ of my pencil is sharp.

(4) He threw the ___anchor___ into the sea.

(5) A ___chicken___ lays eggs.

(6) A tornado can ___destroy___ a building.

You got it!

4

Date 4/29/21 Name Gabriel

Score 100 /100

1 Trace each word. Then read it aloud.

3 points each

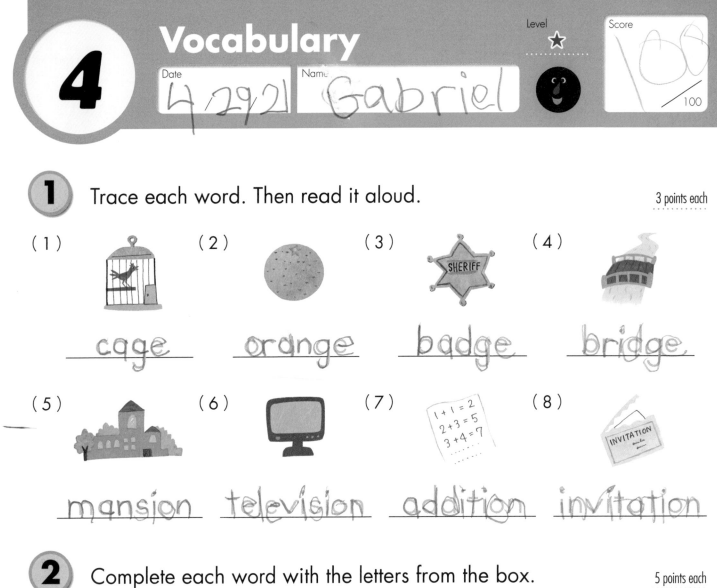

(1) cage

(2) orange

(3) badge

(4) bridge

(5) mansion

(6) television

(7) addition

(8) invitation

2 Complete each word with the letters from the box.

5 points each

| ge | dge | tion | sion |

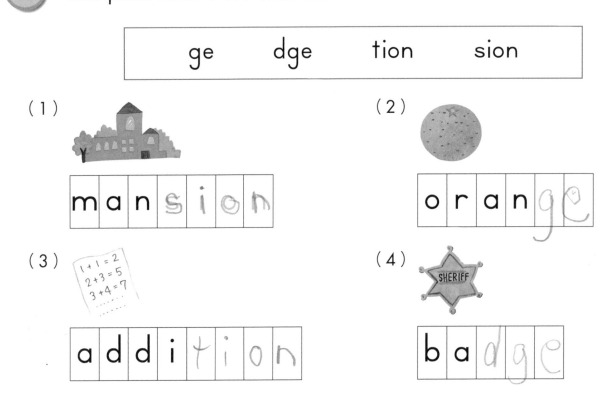

(1) m a n s i o n

(2) o r a n g e

(3) a d d i t i o n

(4) b a d g e

3 Trace the missing letters. Then write the missing word.

4 points each

(1)

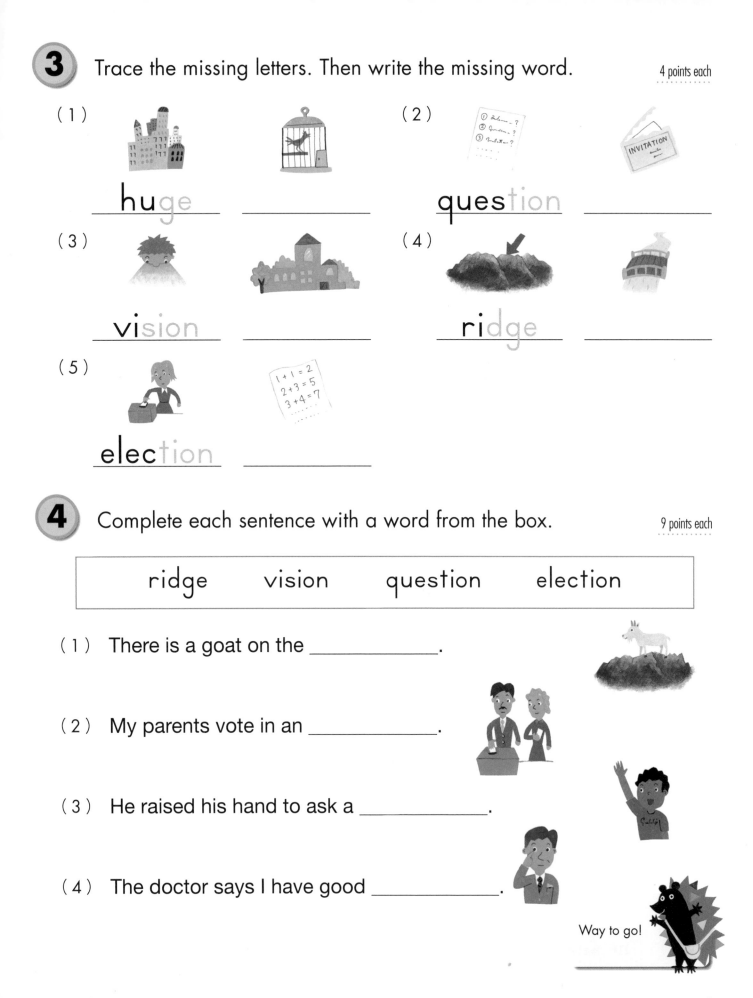

hu_ge_ _____

(2)

ques_tion_ _____

(3)

vi_sion_ _____

(4)

ri_dge_ _____

(5)

elec_tion_ _____

4 Complete each sentence with a word from the box.

9 points each

| ridge | vision | question | election |

(1)   There is a goat on the _____ .

(2)   My parents vote in an _____ .

(3)   He raised his hand to ask a _____ .

(4)   The doctor says I have good _____ .

Way to go!

9

Pronouns

Review

5

Level ☆

Score

/ 100

Date / /

Name

1 Trace the pronoun or pronouns to complete each sentence.   5 points each

(1) __He__ plays the piano. __She__ likes to sing.

(2) __I__ love stories. __You__ have a book.
      Will __you__ read to __me__ ?

(3) __We__ call __them__ over to play.

(4) Did you climb the hill? __It__ is big!

(5) The penguins are funny. __They__ slip and slide.

(6) The dog followed __him__ to the store.
      The cat followed __her__ to the park.

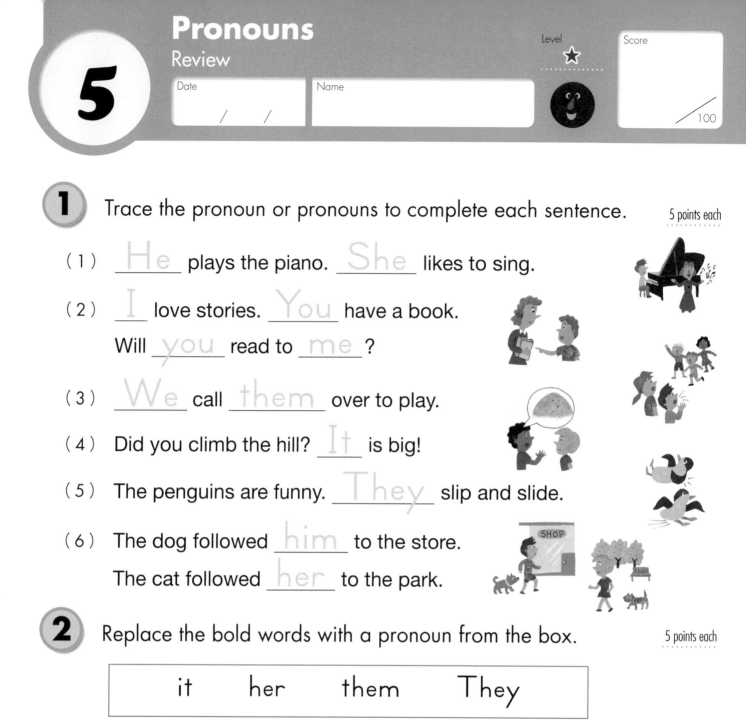

SHOP

2 Replace the bold words with a pronoun from the box.   5 points each

it	her	them	They

(1) Quick! Catch **the runners**!   Quick! Catch ⬚⬚⬚⬚ !

(2) Did you ask **your aunt**?   Did you ask ⬚⬚⬚ ?

(3) She wanted to buy **the robot**.   She wanted to buy ⬚⬚ .

(4) **The students** are taking a test.   ⬚⬚⬚⬚ are taking a test.

3 Complete each sentence with a pronoun.

(1) Bobbie is very tired. ☐☐ will take a nap.

(2) My shoe is untied. I can tie ☐☐ .

(3) Tina and I walk to school.
☐☐ like to skip there, too.

(4) John and Sophia go to the store.
☐☐☐ will buy a present.

(5) Mindy asked for a snack. ☐☐ was hungry.

(6) Can you ride with me?
☐ am scared of roller coasters!

(7) Brenda wanted to tell Jack a secret.
She whispered to ☐☐ .

(8) My teacher gave me an A!
☐ worked hard on my project.

(9) It is Jenni's birthday.
I got ☐☐ a present.

(10) I love playing the piano.
Do ☐☐ like it, too?

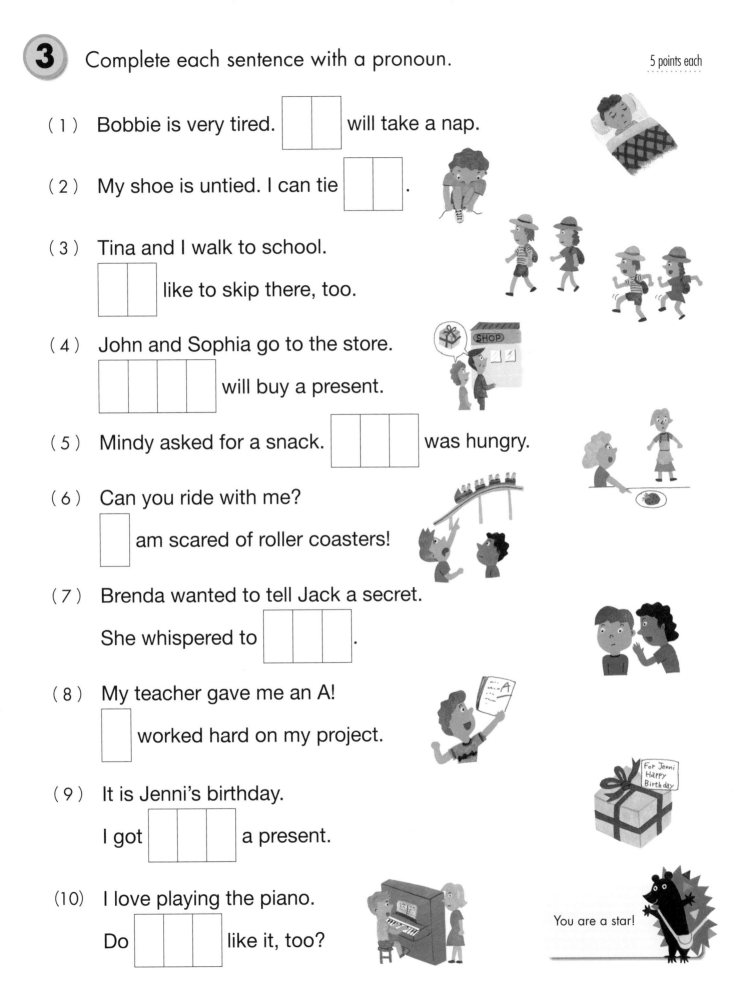

For Jenni
Happy
Birthday

You are a star!

1 Trace the pronoun to complete each sentence.

6 points each

(1) I like _this_ better than your flavor.

(2) _That_ is our car over there.

(3) Barry and I make a snowman.

Ezra comes to help _us_ .

(4) Look at all the birdhouses.

This is Ciara's birdhouse.

(5) Jerry had to go home, but

he wanted to stay with _us_ .

2 Replace the bold words with a pronoun from the box. You can use each pronoun more than once.

5 points each

us	this	that

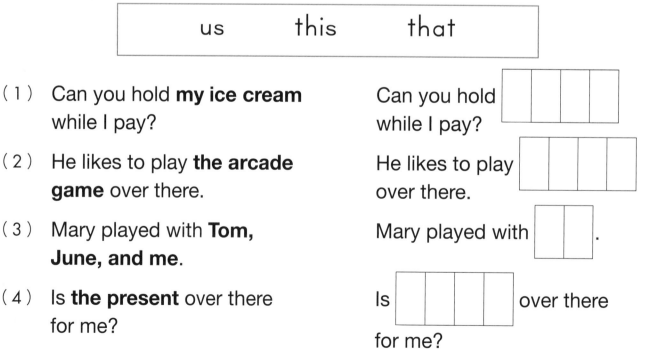

(1) Can you hold **my ice cream** while I pay?

Can you hold [ ] while I pay?

(2) He likes to play **the arcade game** over there.

He likes to play [ ] over there.

(3) Mary played with **Tom, June, and me**.

Mary played with [ ] .

(4) Is **the present** over there for me?

Is [ ] over there for me?

3   Trace the pronoun to complete each sentence.   5 points each

(1)   This is __my__ bag.

      It has __my__ name on it.

(2)   The yellow sweater inside is __mine__ , too.

      Yellow is __my__ favorite color.

(3)   That is __your__ bag. It is not __mine__ .

      It has __your__ name on it.

(4)   The green sweater inside is __yours__ .

      Green is __your__ favorite color.

This is my bag.

4   Complete each sentence with a pronoun.   5 points each

(1)   Is that ☐☐☐☐ room? Can we go in it?

(2)   I tripped because ☐☐ shoe was untied.

(3)   Did you write your name on ☐☐☐☐ project?

(4)   These toys are ☐☐☐ , but I can share them.

(5)   The mess was ☐☐☐ , so I cleaned it up.

(6)   This plate is mine, and that

      plate is ☐☐☐☐☐ .

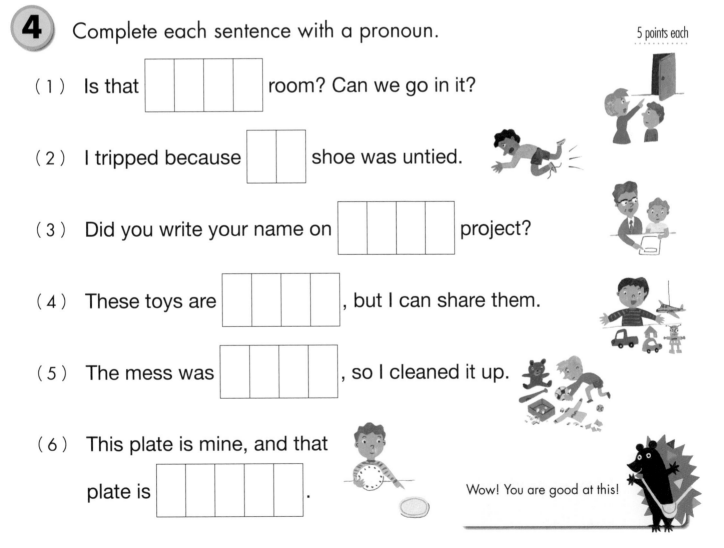

Wow! You are good at this!

  13

Pronouns

7

Date   /   /

Name

Level ☆

Score   /100

---

1 Trace the pronoun to complete each sentence.   5 points each

(1) Chris put on ___his___ hat.

(2) Nikki loves ___her___ pet dog.

(3) That quarter is ___hers___ .

(4) The store opened ___its___ door.

(5) Do not come into ___our___ fort!

(6) Is this car ___ours___ ?

(7) Napping is ___their___ favorite activity.

(8) The ball is ___theirs___ .

---

2 Complete each sentence with a pronoun from the brackets.   5 points each

(1) Come to _____ classroom.   [our / ours]

(2) The science project is _____.   [her / hers]

(3) The robot lifted _____ arm.   [his / its]

(4) They shared _____ snack with me.

[their / theirs]

14   © Kumon Publishing Co., Ltd.

3 Complete each sentence with a pronoun.

(1) The parents watched us in ☐☐☐ school play.

(2) That dog has buried ☐☐☐ toy.

(3) We listen to the singers.

☐☐☐☐☐ singing is very good.

(4) The pizza is ☐☐☐ to share.

(5) Those markers are ☐☐☐☐☐ .

We will use these markers.

(6) Sophie puts polka dots on anything that

is ☐☐☐☐ .

(7) My mom asked me to hold ☐☐☐ hand

while we crossed the street.

(8) Tony is a great writer.

Did you read ☐☐☐ story?

You rock at pronouns!

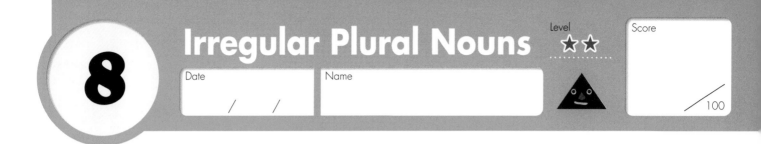

Irregular Plural Nouns

8

Level ★★

Date / /

Name

Score /100

1 Complete the chart by tracing the plural nouns. Then read each noun aloud to hear how the noun changes.

20 points for completion

One / Singular	More than one / Plural
hero	heroes
bush	bushes
glass	glasses

One / Singular	More than one / Plural
berry	berries
penny	pennies
family	families

2 Complete each sentence with the plural form of the noun in the brackets.

5 points each

(1) They wash the [   ].   [glass]

(2) I drop a few [   ].   [penny]

(3) Our [   ] watch us.   [family]

(4) I read about my [   ].   [hero]

(5) A bear ran out of the [   ].   [bush]

(6) Do you like [   ] ?   [berry]

3 Complete the chart by tracing the plural nouns. Then read each noun aloud to hear how the noun changes.

20 points for completion

One / Singular	More than one / Plural	One / Singular	More than one / Plural
witch	witches	puppy	puppies
potato	potatoes	party	parties
tomato	tomatoes	story	stories

4 Complete each sentence with the plural form of the noun in the brackets.

5 points each

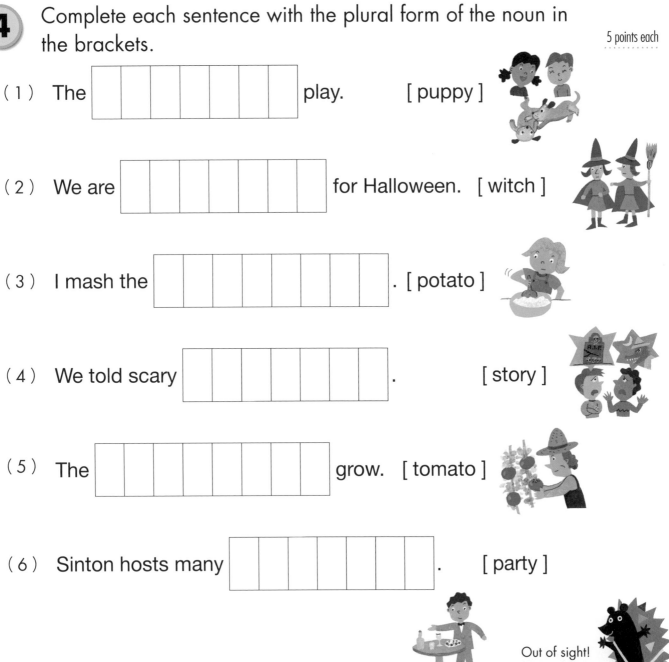

(1) The ⬚⬚⬚⬚⬚⬚⬚ play. [puppy]

(2) We are ⬚⬚⬚⬚⬚⬚ for Halloween. [witch]

(3) I mash the ⬚⬚⬚⬚⬚⬚⬚⬚. [potato]

(4) We told scary ⬚⬚⬚⬚⬚⬚. [story]

(5) The ⬚⬚⬚⬚⬚⬚ grow. [tomato]

(6) Sinton hosts many ⬚⬚⬚⬚⬚⬚. [party]

Out of sight!

17

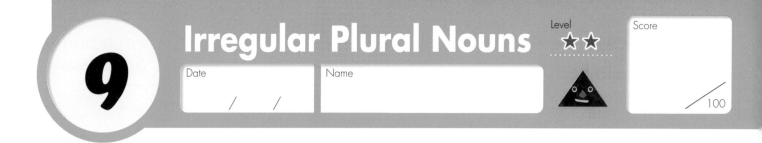
1 Complete the chart by tracing the plural nouns. Then read each noun aloud to hear how the noun changes.

20 points for completion

One / Singular	More than one / Plural	One / Singular	More than one / Plural
child	children	foot	feet
man	men	goose	geese
woman	women	tooth	teeth

2 Complete each sentence with the plural form of the noun in the brackets.

5 points each

(1) I put my ⬚⬚⬚ in the water.   [foot]

(2) The ⬚⬚ got presents on Father's Day.   [man]

(3) The ⬚⬚⬚ were flying South.   [goose]

(4) All the ⬚⬚⬚ wore pretty hats.   [woman]

(5) The ⬚⬚⬚⬚⬚ watch the pony. [child]

(6) Every night, I brush my ⬚⬚⬚⬚ .   [tooth]

3 Complete the chart by tracing the plural nouns. Then read each noun aloud to hear how the noun changes.

20 points for completion

One / Singular	More than one / Plural	One / Singular	More than one / Plural
deer	deer	leaf	leaves
fish	fish	thief	thieves
series	series	loaf	loaves

4 Complete each sentence with the plural form of the noun in the brackets.

5 points each

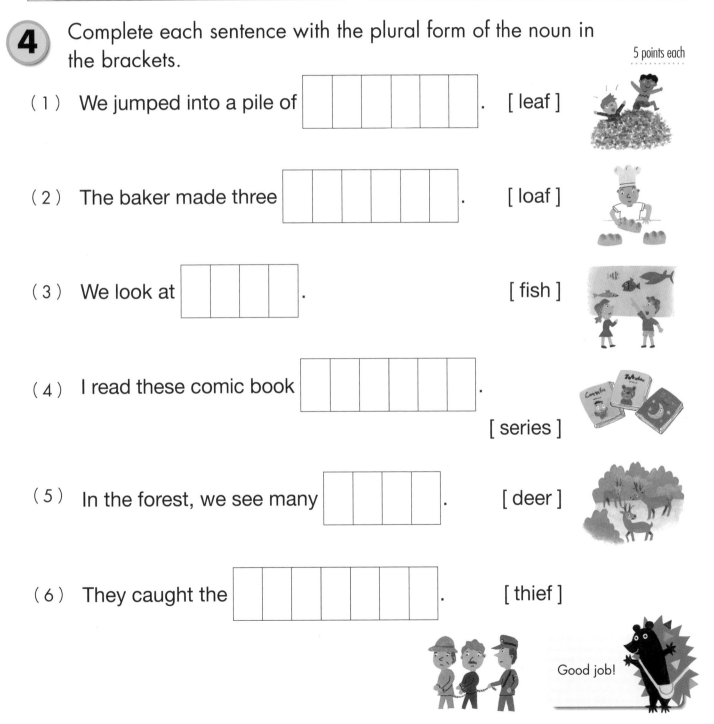

(1) We jumped into a pile of ⬚⬚⬚⬚⬚. [leaf]

(2) The baker made three ⬚⬚⬚⬚⬚. [loaf]

(3) We look at ⬚⬚⬚⬚. [fish]

(4) I read these comic book ⬚⬚⬚⬚⬚. [series]

(5) In the forest, we see many ⬚⬚⬚⬚. [deer]

(6) They caught the ⬚⬚⬚⬚⬚⬚⬚. [thief]

Good job!

Verbs
Review

10

Level ⭐⭐

Date / /

Name

Score

/100

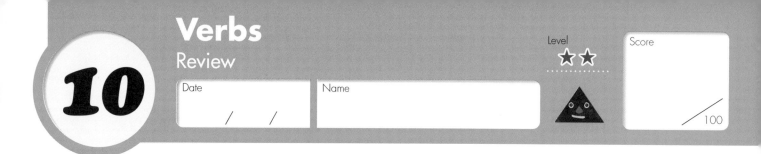

1 Trace the verb to complete each sentence.

6 points each

(1) The fans _cheer_ for the team.

(2) We _visit_ the zoo.

(3) I _land_ on the ground.

(4) Please _open_ this jar for me.

(5) The marbles _scatter_ all over the ground.

Hint: If something is happening *now*, the verb is in the **present** tense. If something has happened *before*, the verb is in the **past** tense. Usually, verbs in the past tense end in "ed."

2 Trace the verb to complete each sentence.

5 points each

(1) I _return_ books to the library.

Earlier, I _returned_ *Days with Frog and Toad*.

(2) Now, you _answer_ the door.

You _answered_ the telephone yesterday.

(3) I _earn_ money each week as a paperboy.

Last week, I _earned_ thirty dollars.

(4) I always _match_ my shoes and shirt.

Yesterday I _matched_ green shoes with a green shirt.

3 Complete each sentence with a verb from the brackets.

6 points each

(1) The sailors _____ the boat safely on shore every day.

[land / landed]

(2) Earlier, the cheerleader _____ from the sidelines.

[cheer / cheered]

(3) The workers _____ the store each day at nine o'clock.

[open / opened]

(4) Each spring, I _____ seeds in the yard.

[scatter / scattered]

(5) I always _____ the giraffe when we go to the zoo.

[visit / visited]

4 Rewrite each sentence in the past tense. End the sentence with a period.

5 points each

(1) I answer the telephone.

_____

(2) We return empty bottles for recycling.

_____

(3) We match our clothes.

_____

(4) The workers earn fifty dollars.

_____

You go the extra mile!

1 Trace each verb to complete each sentence. Then read each sentence aloud.

6 points each

(1) I ___laugh___ at the television show. He ___laughs___ at the clown. Yesterday, they ___laughed___ at the joke.

(2) I ___warm___ the milk. She ___warms___ some hot chocolate. This morning, he ___warmed___ his oatmeal.

(3) You ___travel___ a lot. The pilot ___travels___ everywhere. Last year, we ___traveled___ to Jamaica.

(4) I ___shiver___ during the winter. The dog ___shivers___ in the rain. We ___shivered___ when we went ice-skating.

(5) They ___repair___ the door. The plumber ___repairs___ the sink. After the storm, we ___repaired___ the house.

2 Complete each sentence with a verb from the brackets.

5 points each

(1) Last week, I _____ to see my aunt.
[travel / travels / traveled]

(2) They _____ every time I tell a joke.
[laugh / laughs / laughed]

(3) She _____ the leftovers an hour ago.
[warm / warms / warmed]

(4) I _____ the computers whenever they break.
[repair / repairs / repaired]

3 Trace each verb to complete each sentence. Then read each sentence aloud.

5 points each

(1) Yesterday, we _enjoyed_ a movie. Today, I _enjoy_ a book. My little sister _enjoys_ drawing.

(2) Does a ghost _haunt_ that house? Sometimes a ghost _haunts_ an attic. A ghost _haunted_ our house for years.

(3) I _entertain_ people by dancing. A dancer _entertains_ a crowd. No one _entertained_ us earlier.

(4) I _overflow_ the bathtub by accident. During a flood, the river _overflows_ . Last week, the sink _overflowed_ .

4 Complete each sentence with a verb from the box.

6 points each

| enjoyed   overflows   haunts   enjoys   entertain |

(1) I _____ the tennis match yesterday.

(2) You _____ the party by juggling.

(3) He _____ cooking big meals for his family.

(4) When you pour too much milk, it _____ .

(5) The ghost _____ the cemetery.

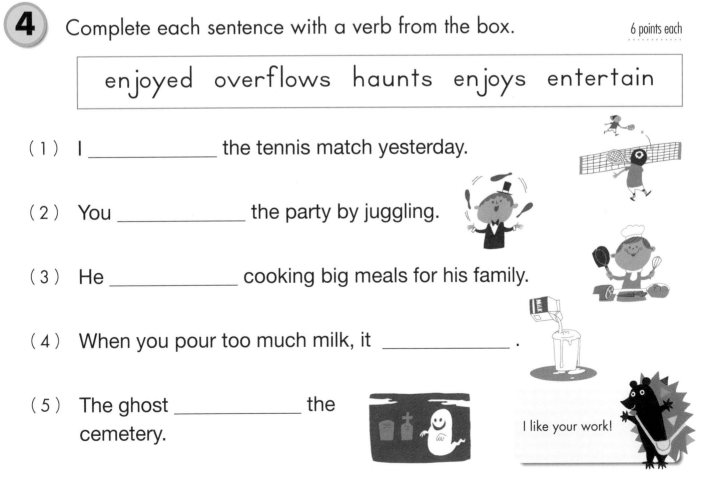

I like your work!

Verbs
Present and Past Tense

12

Level ☆☆

Score

Date / /

Name

/100

1 Trace each verb. Then match the two halves of each sentence.

5 points each

(1) Last Tuesday, the boy •

• performed in a play.

(2) Today, the delivery man •

• borrow a basketball and play a game!

(3) Last week, she •

• collected cans for recycling.

(4) Let us •

• knocks on the door.

2 Complete each sentence with a verb from the box.

5 points each

| borrowed | collect | performs | knocked |

(1) She _____ in an opera.

(2) The kids _____ donations for the animal shelter.

(3) I _____ my older brother's coat and stained it.

(4) At the bowling alley, he _____ all the pins down!

3 Complete each sentence with a verb from the brackets. 6 points each

(1) Yesterday, the newspaper _____ an article about my school. [print / prints / printed]

(2) Do not _____ us into a bush! [steer / steers / steered]

(3) That truck _____ cars every Monday. [transport / transports / transported]

(4) Last week, he _____ to be a pirate. [pretend / pretends / pretended]

(5) My sister _____ her hair when she is nervous. [twist / twists / twisted]

4 Complete each sentence with a verb from the box. 6 points each

| prints | steers | transported | pretend | twist |

(1) Let us _____ to be princesses!

(2) The school _____ report cards for each student.

(3) The driver _____ the fast car.

(4) Earlier today, the mother lion _____ the cub in her mouth.

(5) At gymnastics class, I _____ and turn on the balance beam.

Very clever!

Plural Verbs
Review

13

Level ☆☆

Score /100

Date / /

Name

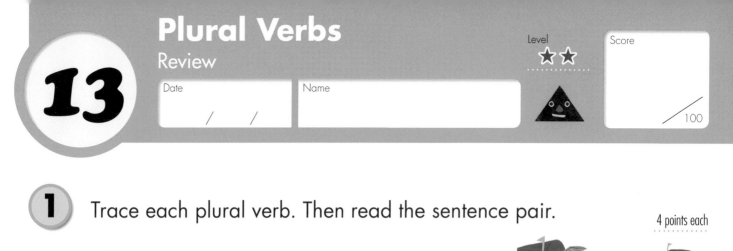

1 Trace each plural verb. Then read the sentence pair.

4 points each

(1) The newspaper arrives.

The newspapers __arrive__ .

(2) The icicle freezes outside.

The icicles __freeze__ outside.

(3) He offers me a sandwich.

They __offer__ me sandwiches.

(4) The boy connects the train cars.

The boys __connect__ the train cars.

(5) The bird-watcher listens for chirping.

The bird-watchers __listen__ for chirping.

> **Don't forget!**
> When the subject of the sentence (the person or thing doing the action) is plural, the verb also must be plural. Most plural verbs do not have an "s" at the end.
> For example: The dog *sleeps*. / The dogs *sleep*.

2 Match the two halves of each sentence.

5 points each

(1) The clown •   • connects the puzzle pieces.

(2) The clowns •   • arrives at the party.

(3) The child •   • connect the puzzle pieces.

(4) The children •   • arrive at the party.

3 Complete each sentence with a verb from the brackets. 6 points each

(1)   The boy _____ the paper together.

[paste / pastes]

(2)   The children _____ the classroom.

[leave / leaves]

(3)   They _____ the bread.

[toast / toasts]

(4)   Ciara and Max _____ on the paper.

[scribble / scribbles]

(5)   She _____ the doll's hair.

[comb / combs]

4 Complete each sentence with the plural form of the verb. 6 points each

(1)   The child scribbles on her drawing pad.

The children _____ on their drawing pads.

(2)   Allison leaves for her vacation.

Gary and Allison _____ for their vacation.

(3)   The camper toasts her marshmallows.

The campers _____ their marshmallows.

(4)   The barber combs a lot of hair every day.

The barbers _____ a lot of hair every day.

(5)   The worker pastes the wallpaper on the wall.

The workers _____ the wallpaper
on the wall.

You are tops!

Plural Verbs

14

Level ☆☆

Date / /

Name

Score /100

1 Complete the chart by tracing the plural nouns and verbs. Then read the words aloud.

15 points for completion

One / Singular	More than one / Plural
I am	We are
You are	You are

One / Singular	More than one / Plural
He is	They are
She is	They are
It is	They are

2 Complete each sentence with a verb from the brackets.

5 points each

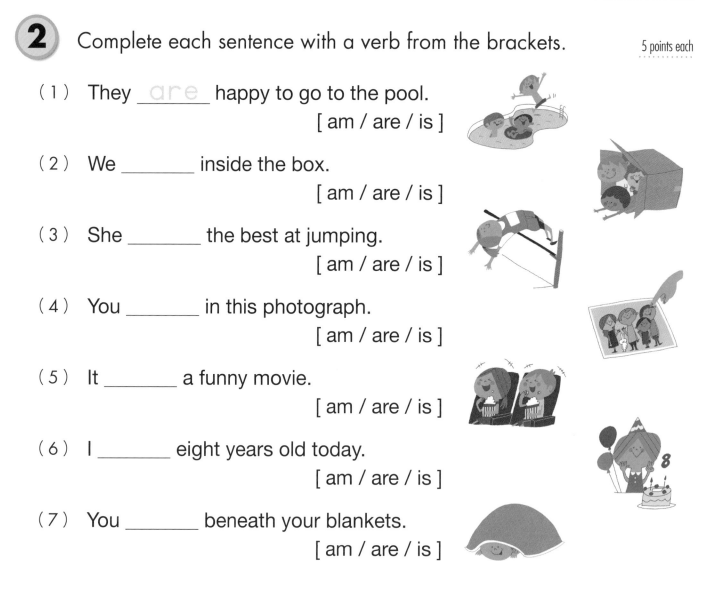

(1) They ___are___ happy to go to the pool.
[am / are / is]

(2) We _____ inside the box.
[am / are / is]

(3) She _____ the best at jumping.
[am / are / is]

(4) You _____ in this photograph.
[am / are / is]

(5) It _____ a funny movie.
[am / are / is]

(6) I _____ eight years old today.
[am / are / is]

(7) You _____ beneath your blankets.
[am / are / is]

28   © Kumon Publishing Co., Ltd.

3 Complete the chart by tracing the plural nouns and verbs. Then read the words aloud.

15 points for completion

One / Singular	More than one / Plural
I have	We have
You have	You have

One / Singular	More than one / Plural
He has	They have
She has	They have
It has	They have

4 Complete each sentence with a verb from the brackets.

5 points each

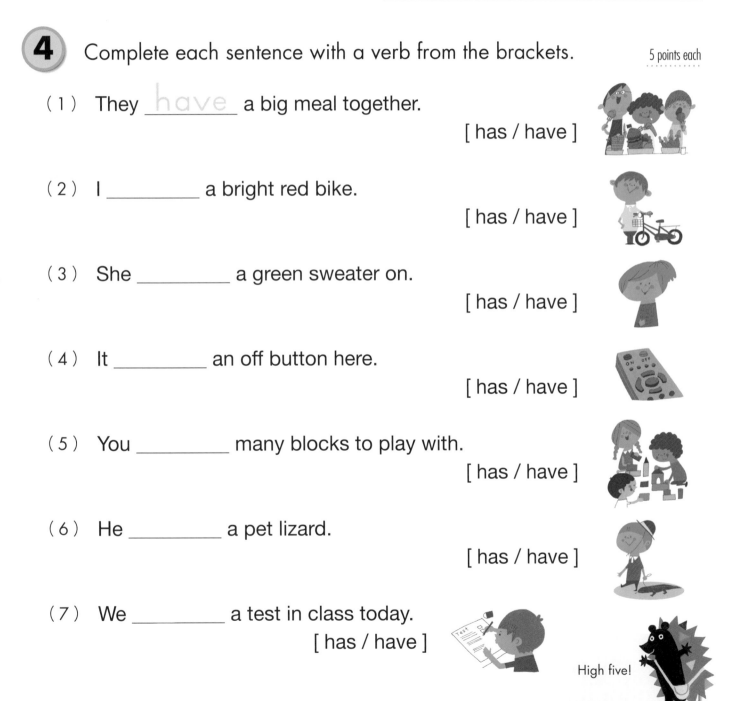

(1) They ___have___ a big meal together.

[has / have]

(2) I _____ a bright red bike.

[has / have]

(3) She _____ a green sweater on.

[has / have]

(4) It _____ an off button here.

[has / have]

(5) You _____ many blocks to play with.

[has / have]

(6) He _____ a pet lizard.

[has / have]

(7) We _____ a test in class today.

[has / have]

High five!

Irregular Verbs

1 Trace the verb to complete each sentence.   5 points each

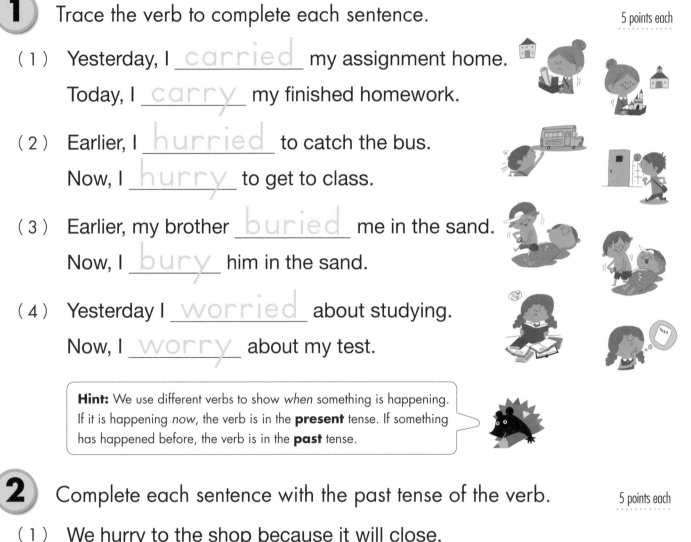

(1) Yesterday, I ___carried___ my assignment home.
Today, I ___carry___ my finished homework.

(2) Earlier, I ___hurried___ to catch the bus.
Now, I ___hurry___ to get to class.

(3) Earlier, my brother ___buried___ me in the sand.
Now, I ___bury___ him in the sand.

(4) Yesterday I ___worried___ about studying.
Now, I ___worry___ about my test.

Hint: We use different verbs to show *when* something is happening. If it is happening *now*, the verb is in the **present** tense. If something has happened before, the verb is in the **past** tense.

2 Complete each sentence with the past tense of the verb.   5 points each

(1) We hurry to the shop because it will close.
We _____ to the shop because it was about to close.

(2) The dogs bury their bones in the backyard now.
The dogs _____ their bones in the backyard earlier.

(3) The nurses worry about me because I am sick.
The nurses _____ about me because I was sick.

(4) The old ships carry many people.
A long time ago, the old ships _____ many people.

3 Trace the verb to complete each sentence.

(1) Today, the boys ___spy___ a very rare bird.

Yesterday, they ___spied___ a beaver.

(2) I ___try___ new food any chance I get.

I ___tried___ clams last week.

(3) I ___reply___ when the teacher calls on me.

I ___replied___ yesterday with the correct answer.

(4) In the movie, the woman and man ___marry___.

My parents ___married___ a long time ago.

(5) The art teachers ___supply___ us with paint.

Last week, they ___supplied___ us with chalk.

4 Complete each sentence with the past tense of the verb.

6 points each

(1) The players try a different plan.
Yesterday, the soccer team _____ to win.

(2) I reply to my pen pal whenever she writes.
I _____ earlier this week.

(3) The girls spy on their older brother.
This morning they _____ on him from the tree house.

(4) Many people marry in this garden.
That couple _____ last week.

(5) The bakers supply the restaurant with treats.
Yesterday, the bakery _____ cakes.

You did great!

31

Irregular Verbs

16

Date　　/　　/

Name

Level ★★

Score ／100

1 Complete the chart by tracing the past tense verbs. Then read each verb aloud to hear how the verb changes.

25 points for completion

Present	Past
bring / brings	brought
think / thinks	thought
buy / buys	bought
teach / teaches	taught
catch / catches	caught

2 Complete each sentence with the past tense of the verb.

5 points each

(1) He teaches us how to fly a kite.

He _____ us how to fly a kite last summer.

(2) She thinks about becoming a doctor.

She _____ about her future.

(3) I bring my grandmother flowers every day.

I _____ my grandmother flowers for her birthday last week.

(4) Spencer catches the foul ball.

Spencer _____ the ball yesterday.

(5) We buy groceries for dinner.

We _____ the groceries for dinner.

32　© Kumon Publishing Co., Ltd.

3 Complete the chart by tracing the past tense verbs. Then read each verb aloud to hear how the verb changes.

25 points for completion

Present	Past
ride / rides	rode
drive / drives	drove
write / writes	wrote
break / breaks	broke
freeze / freezes	froze

4 Complete each sentence with the past tense of the verb.

5 points each

(1)   I write to my uncle, and he writes back.

I _____ to my uncle, and he wrote back.

(2)   She breaks her pencil in half.

She _____ her pencil by accident yesterday.

(3)   The puddles freeze because of the cold weather.

The puddles _____ last night.

(4)   He drives the truck all night and arrives in the morning.

He _____ all last night.

(5)   We ride our bicycles to the fair.

We _____ our bicycles there yesterday.

That is perfect!

17 Irregular Verbs

Date / /

Name

Level ★★

Score /100

1 Trace the verb to complete each sentence.

5 points each

(1) Today, I ___cut___ the cloth.

Yesterday, I ___cut___ the string.

(2) Now, I ___fit___ into this shirt.

Last year, my older brother ___fit___ into this shirt.

(3) This year, we ___beat___ the other team in soccer.

Last year, they ___beat___ us.

(4) Today, I ___read___ about United States history.

Yesterday, I ___read___ a fairy tale.

(5) I ___set___ the table for dinner.

Earlier, my sister ___set___ the table for breakfast.

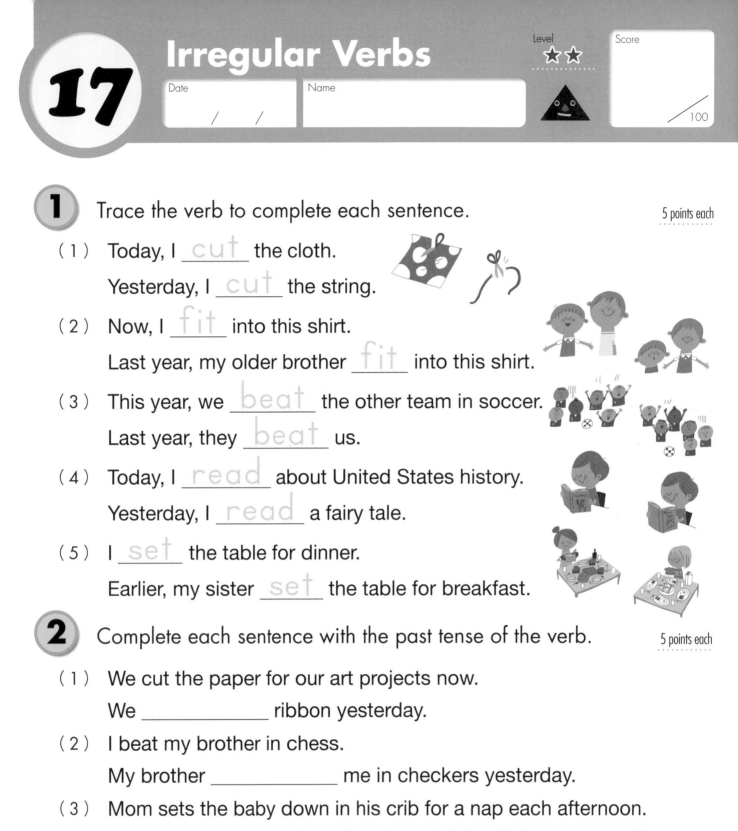

2 Complete each sentence with the past tense of the verb.

5 points each

(1) We cut the paper for our art projects now.

We _____ ribbon yesterday.

(2) I beat my brother in chess.

My brother _____ me in checkers yesterday.

(3) Mom sets the baby down in his crib for a nap each afternoon.

Mom _____ the baby down in his crib for a nap earlier.

(4) I read the weather report every morning.

I _____ the newspaper yesterday.

(5) I fit into the dress.

Last year, I _____ those shoes.

34   © Kumon Publishing Co., Ltd.

3 Trace the verb to complete each sentence.

6 points each

（1） Yesterday, we ___began___ learning about plants.

Today, we ___begin___ the new chapter about life cycles.

（2） This morning, I ___drank___ milk with breakfast.

Now, I ___drink___ water with lunch.

（3） An hour ago, the clock ___rang___ eleven times.

Now, it ___rings___ twelve times.

（4） We ___swam___ in a race last week.

We ___swim___ now for practice.

（5） Yesterday, she ___sang___ a song from the radio.

She ___sings___ in the shower now.

4 Complete each sentence with the past tense of the verb.

5 points each

（1） The athletes swim for an hour.

The athletes _____ for an hour yesterday.

（2） Tonight the concert begins with a slow song.

Last night, the concert _____ with a fast song.

（3） We ring your doorbell to see if you are home.

He _____ your doorbell earlier, but no one was home.

（4） They drink all the lemonade after playing basketball.

She _____ all the lemonade, and now
there is none left.

Radical!

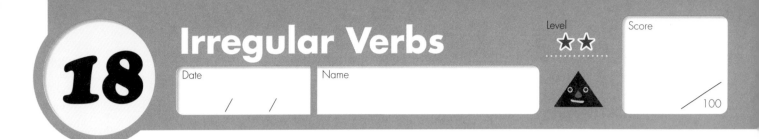

18 Irregular Verbs

1 Complete each chart by tracing the past tense verbs. Then read each verb aloud to hear how the verb changes.

25 points for completion

Present	Past
eat / eats	ate
see / sees	saw
go / goes	went
lead / leads	led
leave / leaves	left

Present	Past
am	was
is	was
are	were
do / does	did
have / has	had

2 Complete each sentence with the past tense of the verb.

5 points each

(1) We go to the zoo.

Yesterday, we _____ to the zoo.

(2) Our scout leader leads us on a hike.

Last week, our scout leader _____ us on a hike.

(3) Jessie eats all the watermelon.

Jessie _____ all of it, so there is none left.

(4) She leaves the city to return to the country.

Last year, she _____ the city to live in the country.

(5) He sees a scary movie.

He _____ a scary movie, so he could not sleep.

3 Complete each sentence with the past tense of the verb. 5 points each

(1) I have my lucky hat on.

I _____ a lucky hat until I lost it.

(2) Mother's Day is in May.

Mother's Day _____ last Sunday.

(3) She is sitting on the steps now.

She _____ sitting, but now she is standing.

(4) They are dancing to the music.

They _____ dancing until the music stopped.

(5) My mom does the cooking on Mondays.

My mom _____ the cooking this morning.

4 Complete each sentence with a verb from the brackets. 5 points each

(1) I _____ older than my sister.   [is / am / was]

(2) Yesterday _____ the last game of the season.

[is / are / was]

(3) We _____ listening to the rain until it stopped.

[is / are / were]

(4) Did you _____ your homework?   [do / did]

(5) She _____ a snack earlier today.

[has / have / had]

Great answers!

19 Contractions

1 Read each word. Then trace the contraction.

20 points for completion

(1) can + not = _can't_

(2) could + not = _couldn't_

(3) is + not = _isn't_

(4) was + not = _wasn't_

(5) do + not = _don't_

(6) did + not = _didn't_

Hint: The words "can" and "not" can also combine to form "cannot."

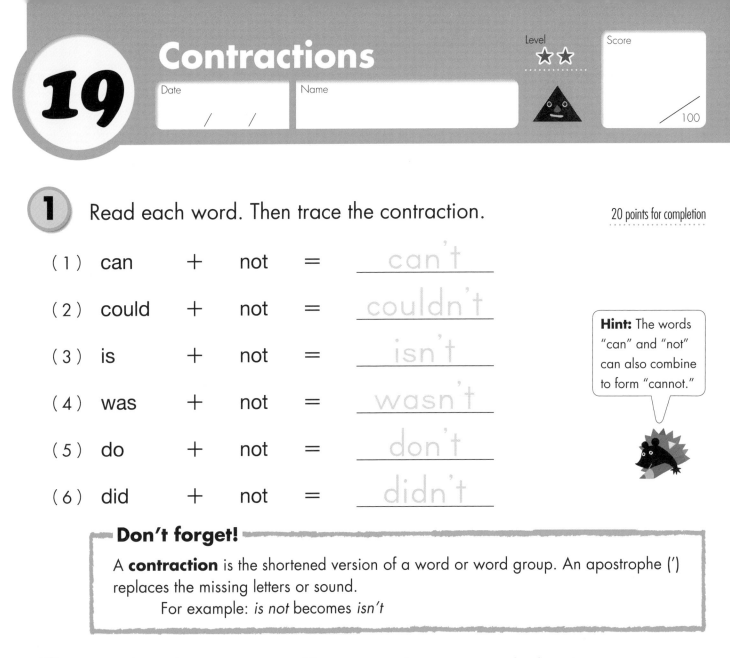

Don't forget!

A **contraction** is the shortened version of a word or word group. An apostrophe (') replaces the missing letters or sound.

For example: *is not* becomes *isn't*

---

2 Read each contraction. Then write the two words that it represents.

20 points for completion

(1) wasn't = _____ + _____

(2) don't = _____ + _____

(3) isn't = _____ + _____

(4) can't = _____ + _____

(5) couldn't = _____ + _____

(6) didn't = _____ + _____

3 Complete each sentence with a word from the brackets.

6 points each

(1) She _____ arrive on time because she was stuck in traffic.

[wasn't / couldn't]

(2) My dad _____ cook dinner. We got pizza instead.

[didn't / don't]

(3) Fried food _____ a healthy choice for lunch.

[can't / isn't]

(4) He _____ jog anymore because he hurt his knee.

[didn't / wasn't]

(5) My brother _____ reach the top shelf, so I help him.

[can't / don't]

4 Complete each sentence with a word from the box.

6 points each

can't	couldn't	wasn't	don't	didn't

(1) I _____ want to get out of bed yesterday.

(2) She _____ happy because her marker ran out of ink.

(3) Anita _____ lift her mom's purse because it was too heavy.

(4) He _____ sing well, so he plays the trumpet.

(5) Please _____ play near a busy street.

Fantastic!

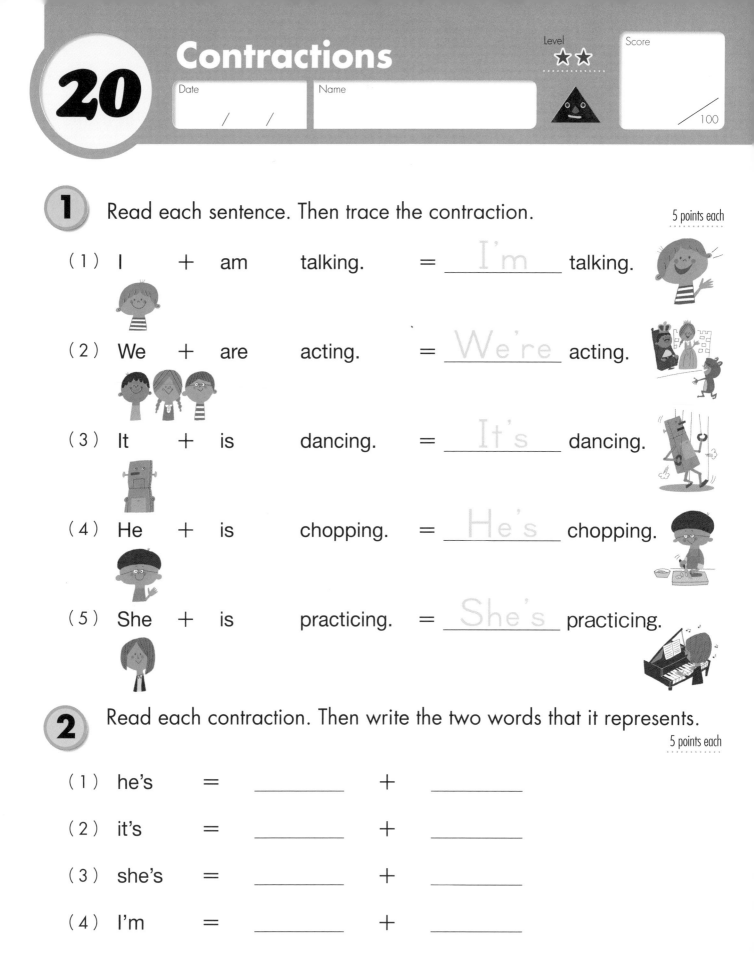

20 Contractions

Level ★★

Score /100

Date / /   Name

1 Read each sentence. Then trace the contraction.

5 points each

(1) I + am talking. = I'm talking.

(2) We + are acting. = We're acting.

(3) It + is dancing. = It's dancing.

(4) He + is chopping. = He's chopping.

(5) She + is practicing. = She's practicing.

2 Read each contraction. Then write the two words that it represents.

5 points each

(1) he's = _____ + _____

(2) it's = _____ + _____

(3) she's = _____ + _____

(4) I'm = _____ + _____

(5) we're = _____ + _____

3 Complete each sentence with a word from the brackets.   5 points each

(1) _____ going together to our family reunion.
[We're / She's]

(2) _____ almost bedtime.
[It's / He's]

(3) _____ happy I found my lost dog.
[I'm / It's]

(4) _____ treating herself to a new shirt.
[She's / We're]

(5) _____ the only person asleep.
[He's / We're]

4 Complete each sentence with a word from the box.   5 points each

I'm We're It's He's She's

(1) _____ hungry for my snack.

(2) _____ a fireman.

(3) _____ singing in a chorus together.

(4) _____ an animal doctor.

(5) _____ a sunny day,
so we can play outside.

You're super!

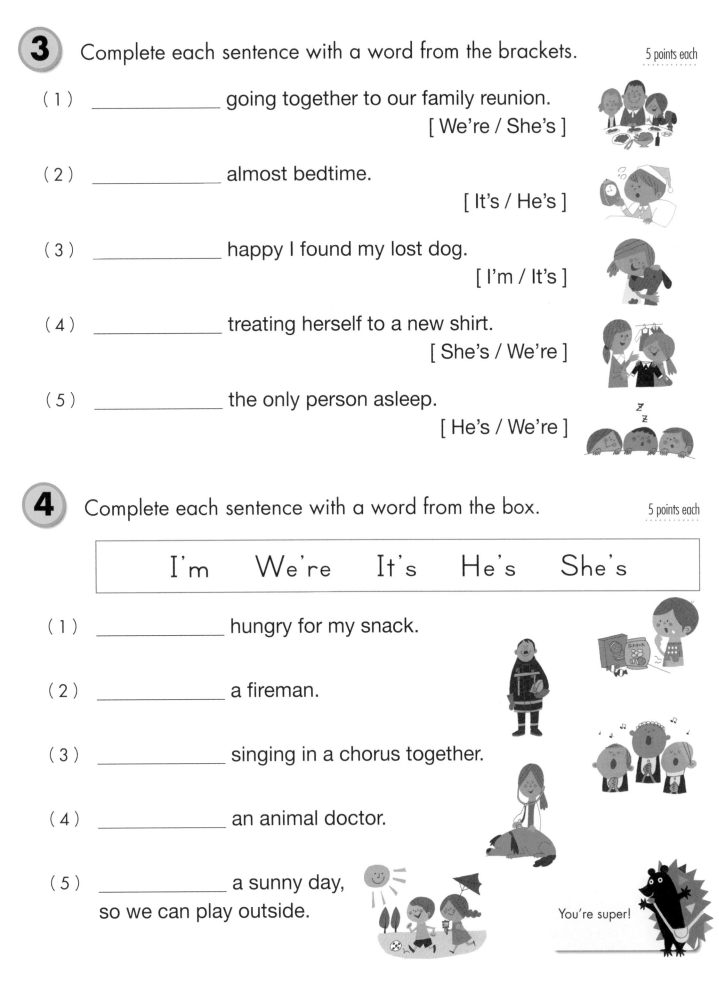

Adjectives

1 Answer each question.

5 points per question

(1) Is the watermelon juicy or dry?

The watermelon is __juicy__ .

(2) Is the market busy or calm?

The market is _____.

(3) Is the road straight or curvy?

The road is _____.

(4) Is the athlete strong or weak?

The athlete is _____.

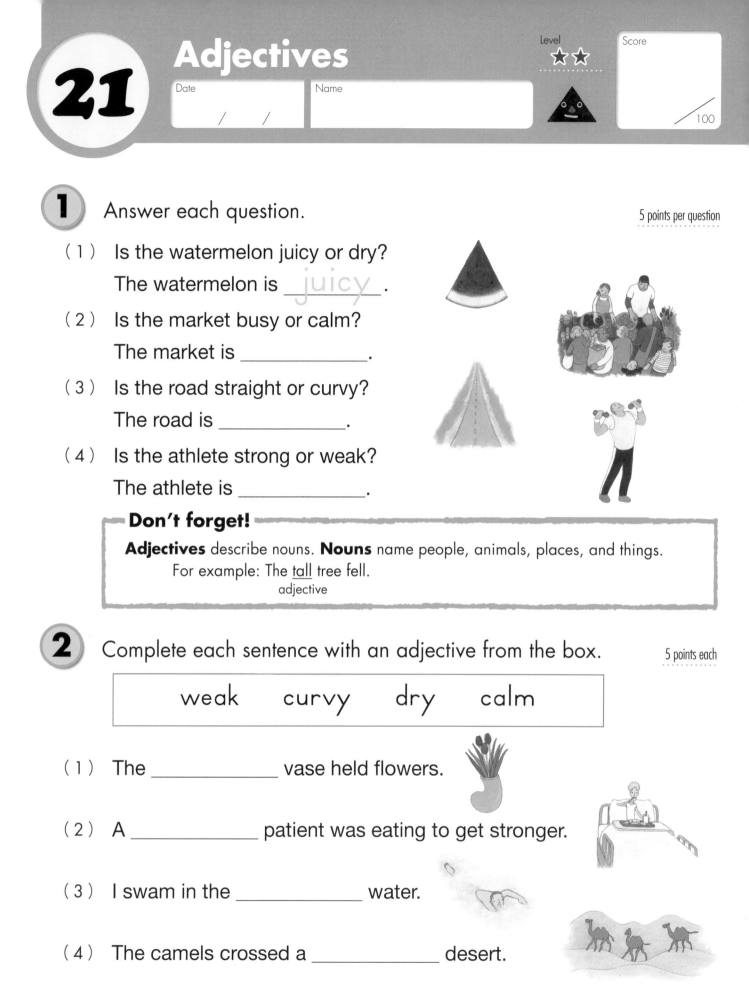

> **Don't forget!**
>
> **Adjectives** describe nouns. **Nouns** name people, animals, places, and things.
> For example: The <u>tall</u> tree fell.
>   adjective

2 Complete each sentence with an adjective from the box.

5 points each

weak	curvy	dry	calm

(1) The _____ vase held flowers.

(2) A _____ patient was eating to get stronger.

(3) I swam in the _____ water.

(4) The camels crossed a _____ desert.

3 Complete the table.

25 points for completion

quick	quicker	quickest
long	_____	longest

_____	brighter	_____
_____	_____	smallest

4 Add "er" to each bold adjective so it means "more than."   5 points each

(1) The nightlight is **bright**, but the lamp

is _____.

(2) My dog is **small**, but my turtle

is _____.

(3) Walking was **quick**, but skateboarding

was _____.

(4) The squirrel's tail was **long**, but the

horse's tail was _____.

5 Complete each sentence with an adjective from the box.   5 points each

brightest   smallest   longest

(1) She chose the _____ dress

for her party.

(2) Don't choose the _____ line

at the supermarket.

(3) She is the _____ of the

puppies.

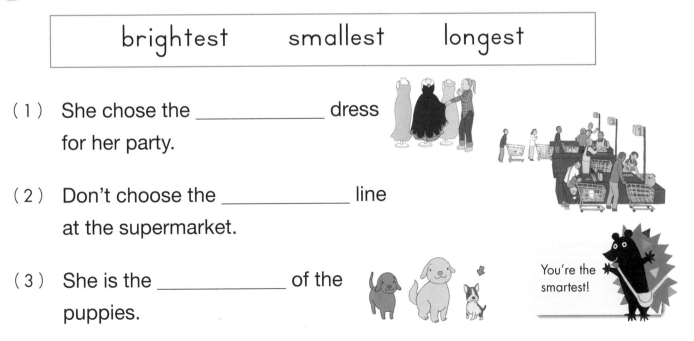

You're the smartest!

Subject and Predicate
Review

22

Level ★★

Date / /

Name

Score

/100

1 Complete each sentence with a subject from the brackets.

6 points each

(1) _____ are reading.
[The boys / Lions]

(2) _____ eats honey. [A bear / The owl]

(3) _____ likes walking.
[A bird / My dog]

(4) _____ scratches the couch.
[Our cat / My brother]

(5) _____ works hard. [Mom / The horse]

> **Don't forget!**
>
> The **subject** is the part of a sentence that tells who or what the sentence is about or who or what is doing the action.
>
> The **predicate** is the part of the sentence that tells what the subject is doing.
>
> For example: <u>The team</u> <u>practiced all day</u>.
>   subject   predicate

2 Match the subject and predicate.

5 points each

(1) Her car •   • chased a mouse.

(2) The cat •   • read two books yesterday.

(3) Cara •   • are coming over.

(4) My friends •   • needs new tires.

3 Write the subject of each sentence in the space provided.   6 points each

(1)   Three girls went to the zoo.   _____

(2)   The lion roared at them fiercely.   _____

(3)   Two giraffes ate leaves
from the trees.   _____

(4)   The zookeeper fed the seals.   _____

(5)   The girls liked the cute monkeys.   _____

4 Complete each sentence with a subject and predicate from
the boxes.   5 points each

Subjects

| Predicates |

My goldfish   A dog
My grandma   Tom

is a good friend   swims all day
lives next door   digs a hole

(1)   _____   _____ .
Subject   Predicate

(2)   _____   _____ .
Subject   Predicate

(3)   _____   _____ .
Subject   Predicate

(4)   _____   _____ .
Subject   Predicate

Well done!

1 Match the subject and predicate.

5 points each

Subject		Predicate
(1) The little black dog ●		● plays baseball.
(2) Grandpa's old car ●		● cleaned the classroom.
(3) An icy wind ●		● cooled on the table.
(4) My kind friend ●		● jumped into the car.
(5) My big brother ●		● won a prize.
(6) The hot apple pie ●		● were on the table.
(7) Mae's fancy dishes ●		● blew off my hat.
(8) Her helpful students ●		● shared his sandwich.

Don't forget!

If an **adjective** describes the **subject**, it is also part of the subject of the sentence.
For example: The loud siren hurt my ears.
subject

2 Write the subject of each sentence in the space provided.

5 points each

(1) The little mouse crept away.

_____ _____ _____

(2) A red rose was in my vase.

_____ _____ _____

(3) Her curly hair was beautiful.

_____ _____ _____

(4) The wet towels were on the floor.

_____ _____ _____

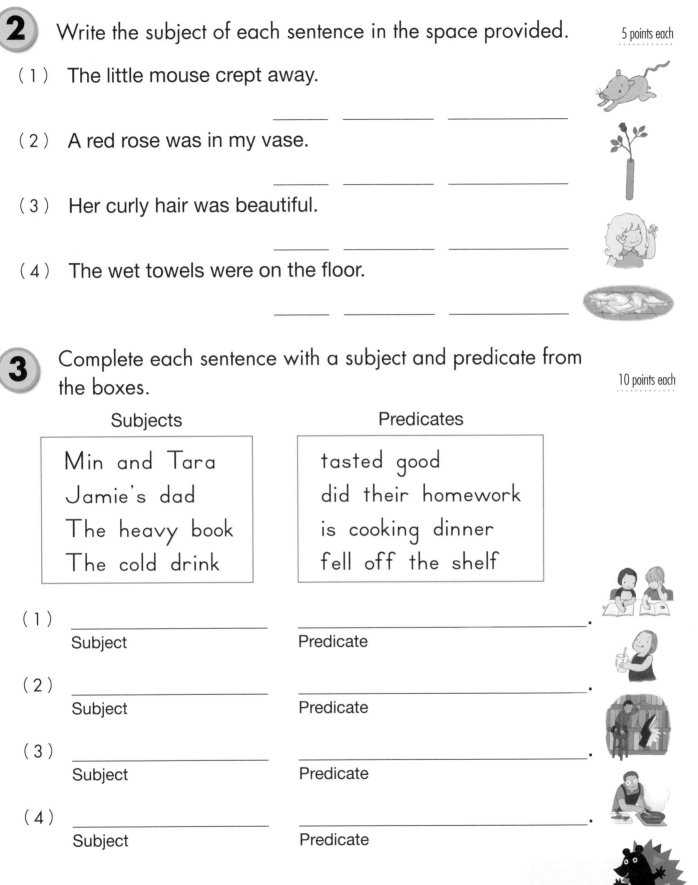

3 Complete each sentence with a subject and predicate from the boxes.

10 points each

Subjects	Predicates
Min and Tara Jamie's dad The heavy book The cold drink	tasted good did their homework is cooking dinner fell off the shelf

(1) _____   _____ .
Subject   Predicate

(2) _____   _____ .
Subject   Predicate

(3) _____   _____ .
Subject   Predicate

(4) _____   _____ .
Subject   Predicate

Keep trying.

24 Longer Subjects

Level ★★★

Date   /   /

Name

Score   /100

---

1 Complete each sentence with an adjective from the brackets.   4 points each

(1) My _____ sweater   hangs in the closet.
       Subject   Predicate   [red / blue]

(2) The _____ baby   fell asleep.
       Subject   Predicate   [hungry / tired]

(3) Her _____ bike   is in the garage.
       Subject   Predicate   [red / blue]

(4) Our _____ bird   loves her new cage.
       Subject   Predicate   [little / big]

---

2 Complete each subject with an adjective from the box.

4 points each

| funny   messy   tall   soft   green |

(1) The _____ clown gave us balloons.

(2) Mom's _____ dress looks great!

(3) Greg's _____ pillow fell off the bed.

(4) The _____ block tower came crashing down.

(5) Our _____ classroom needs to be cleaned.

3 Rewrite each sentence with the adjective in the brackets.

8 points each

(1) The snow   covered the ground.   [white]
Subject

The white snow covered the ground.

(2) The children   went to the zoo.   [excited]
Subject

_____.

(3) Jack's cars   roll everywhere.   [fast]
Subject

_____.

(4) The singer   sang on stage.   [famous]
Subject

_____.

(5) A girl   hid under the table.   [tiny]
Subject

_____.

(6) Two kittens   played in the pet shop.   [cute]
Subject

_____.

(7) Mom's coat   got dirty.   [beautiful]
Subject

_____.

(8) The winner   got a prize.   [lucky]
Subject

_____.

Take a bow!

Adverbs

Date   /   /

Name

Level
★ ★ ★

Score
/ 100

1 Trace the word. Then read each sentence pair aloud.

5 points each

(1)   He ran.

He ran _quickly_ .

(2)   The new golfer hit the ball.

The new golfer hit the ball _badly_ .

(3)   I made my bed.

I made my bed _neatly_ .

(4)   Riku walked home from school.

Riku _slowly_ walked home from school.

> **Don't forget!**
> An **adverb** is a word that describes a verb. Adverbs often end in "ly." Some adverbs tell how an action takes place.
>   For example: Amy happily sang.
>   adverb   verb
>   subject   predicate

2 Complete each sentence with an adverb from the brackets.

5 points each

(1)   The children played _____.

[noisily / quietly]

(2)   Oliver _____ painted his picture.

[lightly / messily]

(3)   The dog _____ ate his food.

[hungrily / gently]

(4)   The man _____ opened his present.

[angrily / happily]

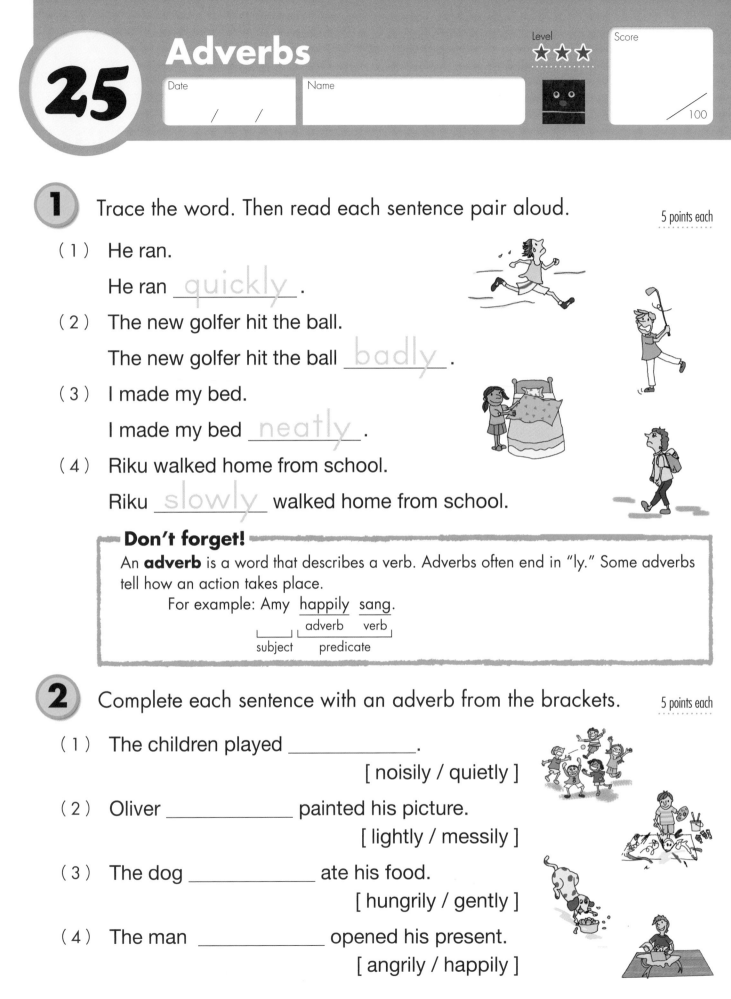

3 Read the sentence and then answer the question.

6 points per question

(1) Callie read quickly in the bookstore.
How did Callie read? Callie read __quickly__ .

(2) We gently pet the kittens at the store.
How did we pet the kittens? We pet the kittens _____ .

(3) Marco danced beautifully during the show.
How did Marco dance? Marco danced _____ .

(4) The cow hungrily ate the grass in the field.
How did the cow eat? The cow ate _____ .

(5) The firefighter acted bravely during the fire.
How did the firefighter act? The firefighter acted _____ .

(6) The umpire yelled angrily at the coach.
How did the umpire yell? The umpire yelled _____ .

(7) The stars shined brightly in the sky.
How did the stars shine? The stars shined _____ .

(8) The girls played messily with the clay.
How did the girls play? The girls played _____ .

(9) The crowd cheered loudly at the end.
How did the crowd cheer? The crowd cheered _____ .

(10) In the library, the people read quietly.
How did the people read? The people read _____ .

Super!

26 Adverbs

1 Trace the adverb to complete each sentence.

5 points each

(1) Tamara _happily_ finished the story.

(2) Eli _skillfully_ drew on his paper.

(3) There will be a test _tomorrow_.

(4) I play _outside_.

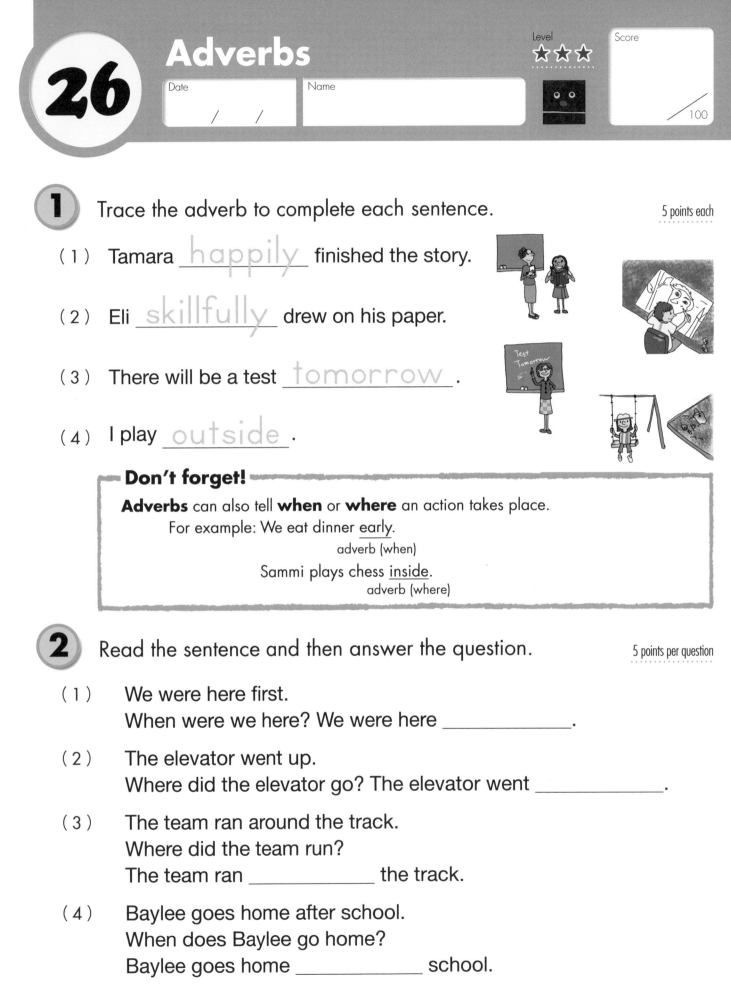

Don't forget!

Adverbs can also tell **when** or **where** an action takes place.
For example: We eat dinner early.
adverb (when)
Sammi plays chess inside.
adverb (where)

---

2 Read the sentence and then answer the question.

5 points per question

(1) We were here first.
When were we here? We were here _____.

(2) The elevator went up.
Where did the elevator go? The elevator went _____.

(3) The team ran around the track.
Where did the team run?
The team ran _____ the track.

(4) Baylee goes home after school.
When does Baylee go home?
Baylee goes home _____ school.

3 Circle the adverb in each sentence.

5 points each

(1)   Dad said we are not going later.

(2)   The kittens hid under the table.

(3)   The remote control fell behind the couch.

(4)   The horse jumped over the fence.

(5)   We went to the market earlier.

 4   Complete the story with the adverbs from the box.

35 points for completion

after   behind   sweetly   quickly

I went for a walk _____ lunch.
I saw something run into the bushes
of my neighbor's yard. It was brown
and furry. I _____ went to see
what it was. I peeked _____
my neighbor's fence. It was a tiny
kitten! It looked up at me
_____ .

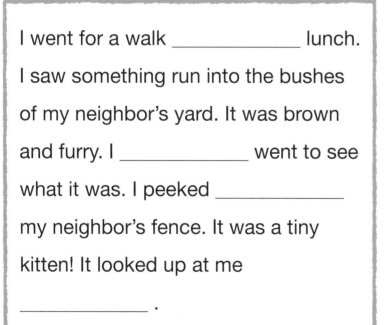

Keep up the good work.

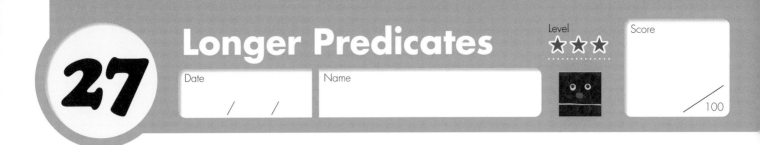

1 Complete each predicate with an adverb from the box.   5 points each

| roughly | before | near | loudly |

(1) She   played the song _____.
       Subject   Predicate

(2) The strong wind   _____ blew the branches.
       Subject   Predicate

(3) The queen's horses   stayed _____ the castle.
       Subject   Predicate

(4) Ben   put on his skates _____ practice.
       Subject   Predicate

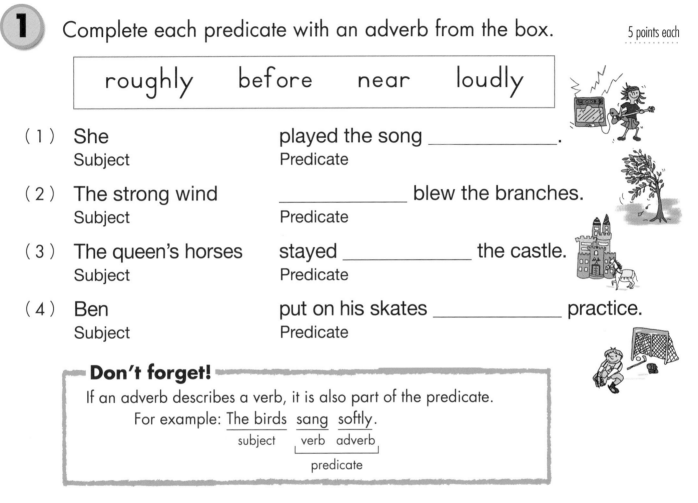

> **Don't forget!**
> If an adverb describes a verb, it is also part of the predicate.
> For example: The birds sang softly.
>   subject   verb adverb
>   predicate

2 Read each sentence. Then write the predicate in the space provided.
                                                              6 points each

(1) Anna will come over later.   will come over later

(2) My friend sings nicely.   _____

(3) Our aunt greeted us warmly.   _____

(4) The girl lost her ring often.   _____

(5) The monkey climbed carefully.   _____

3 Complete each sentence with a predicate from the box.   6 points each

| exercises daily   has an elevator inside   happily live at the zoo |
| will go to school next week   told us to eat healthfully |

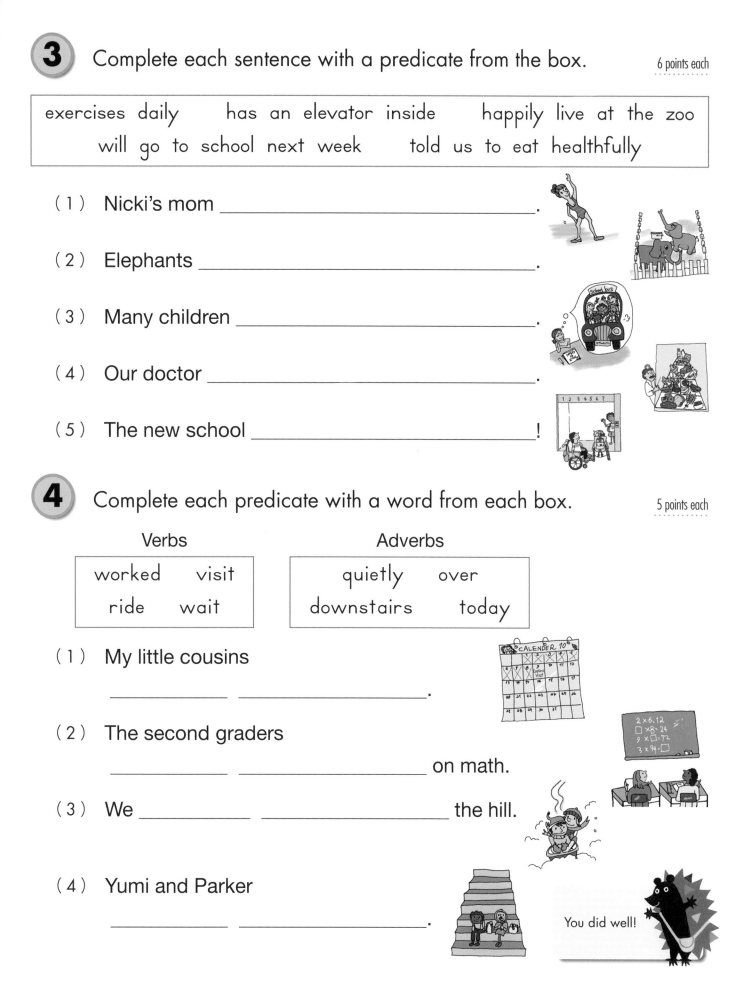

(1) Nicki's mom _____.

(2) Elephants _____.

(3) Many children _____.

(4) Our doctor _____.

(5) The new school _____!

4 Complete each predicate with a word from each box.   5 points each

Verbs

| worked   visit |
| ride   wait |

Adverbs

| quietly   over |
| downstairs   today |

(1) My little cousins

_____ _____.

(2) The second graders

_____ _____ on math.

(3) We _____ _____ the hill.

(4) Yumi and Parker

_____ _____.

You did well!

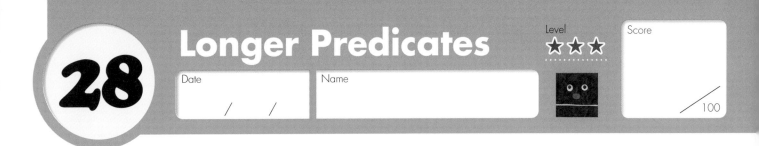

28 Longer Predicates

Date / /

Name

Level ★★★

Score /100

1 Match each subject and predicate.

5 points each

(1) My new classmates ●   ● fit tightly.

(2) His old sweatshirt ●   ● is next in line.

(3) Arjun ●   ● played too roughly.

(4) The soccer players ●   ● greeted me warmly.

2 Complete each sentence with a predicate from the box.

6 points each

closed the jar tightly	had a scratch
will finally ski down	gobbled his food hungrily
live in burrows underground	

(1) Anya and her mother _____.

(2) The shiny bike _____.

(3) The sweet baby _____.

(4) Prairie dogs _____.

(5) I _____.

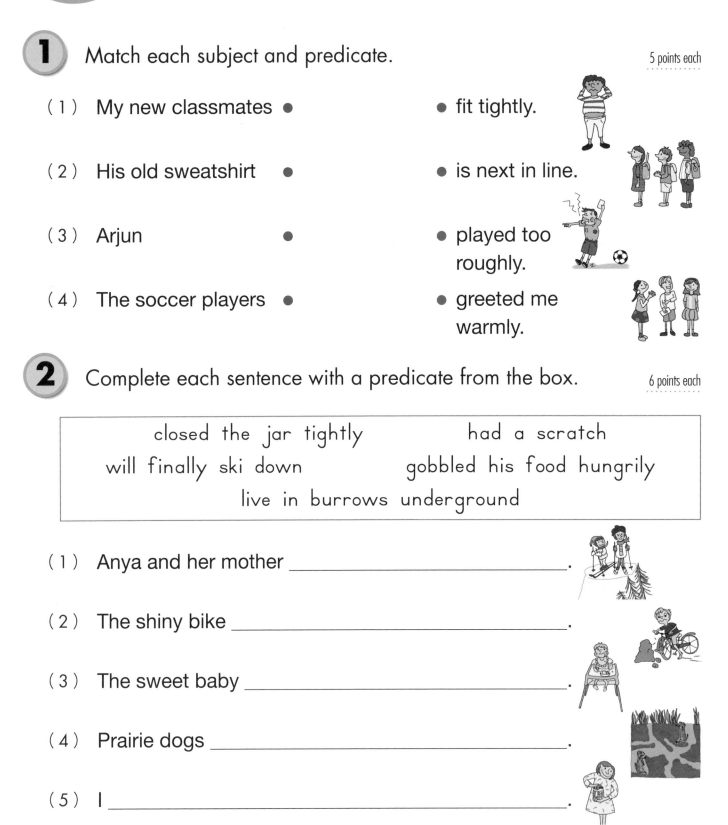

3 Read each sentence. Write the predicate in the space provided.

5 points each

(1) Mom's houseplant sat safely on a high shelf. _____

(2) Julian swung on the monkey bars. _____

(3) Imani went to school cheerfully. _____

(4) The big red dog was very lively. _____

4 Write each sentence with a subject and predicate from the boxes.

6 points each

Subjects	Predicates
The beautiful painting Lucia's gerbil Our neighbors My science projects The snowman	politely waved at us was carried carefully ran under her dresser quickly melted in the sun are up on the wall

(1) _____.

(2) _____.

(3) _____.

(4) _____.

(5) _____.

Great job!

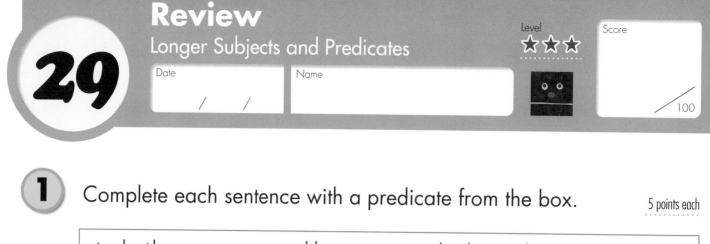

Review
Longer Subjects and Predicates

29

Level ☆☆☆

Date / /

Name

Score /100

1 Complete each sentence with a predicate from the box.

5 points each

> took the money greedily   munched on the grass quietly
> smiled sweetly   is on the bench   stuck to the pan
> pulled the wagon slowly   hid the present upstairs
> drank the milk quickly

(1) Dad's pancakes _____.

(2) The robber _____.

(3) The baby _____.

(4) The tired children _____.

(5) Our parents _____.

(6) Two rabbits _____.

(7) Eva's red jacket _____.

(8) The two sisters _____.

2 Read each sentence aloud. Circle the subject. Then write the predicate in the space provided.

6 points each

(1) A happy little girl digs in the sand.

_____

(2) The huge airplane took off quickly.

_____

(3) The family comes here for a party.

_____

(4) Our art class worked together nicely.

_____

(5) The town's new playground was very crowded.

_____

(6) Jacob washed the dirty clothes.

_____

(7) The children's museum opens early.

_____

(8) Brenden's little yellow backpack was in the car.

_____

(9) The teammates listened to their coach patiently.

_____

(10) The talented singer won many awards.

_____

Nicely done!

30

1 Correct each sentence with a capital letter at the beginning and a period at the end.

4 points each

(1) the bird ate the juicy worm

_____

(2) we have a picnic with our teacher

_____

(3) my cat jumped swiftly onto the table

_____

(4) the cute baby laughed at us

_____

(5) the party starts at three o'clock

_____

2 Complete each question to match the statement. End each question with a question mark.

4 points each

(1) Does ___Mark___ have ___three dogs___ ?
Mark has three dogs.

(2) Where are _____ ___
The colored pencils are in the drawer.

(3) Did _____ do _____ ___
Sue did all her science homework.

(4) Do _____ sing _____ ___
Yes, the birds sing sweetly in the trees.

(5) Are _____ going _____ ___
We are going to the beach this summer.

3 Rewrite each sentence with a capital letter and correct spacing. Complete each sentence with a period, question mark, or exclamation mark.

(1) ourschoolpicnicistoday

Our school picnic is today.

(2) wewillplaygamesandeatoutside

_____

(3) wewillrunrelayraces

_____

(4) watchoutfortherunners

_____

(5) whichclasswontherace

_____

(6) whatwillwehaveforlunch

_____

Do your best.

Punctuation
Quotation Marks

Level ☆☆☆

Score / 100

1 Underline the words and punctuation in each sentence that are between the quotation marks (" ").

5 points each

(1) "Good morning, Mom," said Ava.

(2) "Can I have some more cookies?" asked Jay.

(3) "It is going to be a nice day today," Mrs. Cho said.

(4) "Let's go swimming!" cried the children.

Don't forget!

Quotation marks are used in a sentence to show what someone has said.
Quotation marks are always used in pairs to mark the beginning and end of a quotation.
For example: "Here is my homework," said Omar.
"How are you?" asked Dara.
"What a great day!" exclaimed Dad.

---

2 Read each sentence. Write quotation marks in the boxes around the words that tell what someone has said.

6 points each

(1) ☐ The baby is crying, ☐ said Mom.

(2) ☐ My homework is in my backpack, ☐ said Ramone.

(3) ☐ What did you get for your birthday? ☐ asked Grandpa.

(4) ☐ We won the soccer game! ☐ yelled Iman.

(5) ☐ Where are my new sandals? ☐ asked Chaz.

© Kumon Publishing Co., Ltd.

3 Write each quotation between the two quotation marks to complete the sentence.

5 points each

(1) Here is your birthday present

"Here is your birthday present," said my cousin.

(2) Chocolate chip is my favorite ice cream

"_____," Ali said.

(3) Are we going to miss practice

"_____?" asked Kim.

(4) We had a wonderful time

"_____!" exclaimed Uncle Joe.

4 Rewrite each sentence with quotation marks around the words that tell what someone has said.

6 points each

(1) Gia went back to sleep, said Nana.

"Gia went back to sleep," said Nana.

(2) How old are you? asked the principal.

_____ asked the principal.

(3) We are so happy to see you! exclaimed Kira.

_____ exclaimed Kira.

(4) We will get popsicles today, said Sol.

_____ said Sol.

(5) Please come over to play, said Ron.

_____ said Ron.

This is your best work.

Writing Sentences
Review

32

Level
☆☆☆

Date   /   /

Name

Score
/100

1 Rewrite each sentence with correct spacing and punctuation.   5 points each

(1)   ourfavoriteparkclosedyesterday

_____

(2)   catchthevase

_____

(3)   canwegohome

_____

(4)   thetinydogbarkedangrily

_____

2 Complete each sentence with a word from the box.   4 points each

excited   brightly   wisely   loudly   carefully

(1)   The sun shone _____.

(2)   Nearby, an ice cream truck played

its tune _____.

(3)   The _____ children were

playing games.

(4)   Mom and Dad helped Leo ride

_____.

(5)   Leo _____ wore a helmet.

3 Write each sentence with a subject and predicate from the boxes. Don't forget to capitalize and use proper punctuation.

10 points each

Subjects

the tiny fairy
Hiroshi
Saya and Josh
a brown coyote
the hot soup
Mrs. Bing

Predicates

spilled everywhere
crept in the bushes
flew around merrily
stretch after class
fixed the swing outside
sang the song loudly

(1) _____

(2) _____

(3) _____

(4) _____

(5) _____

(6) _____

You did it!

33 **Writing a Story**

Level ☆☆☆

Score

Date / /

Name

/100

1 Complete the story with adjectives from the box. Then read the story aloud.

5 points each

pretty	salty	red	great	tiny
long	tasty	cold	black	sunny

One (1) __sunny__ day, I went to my friend Dominique's house.

Dominique's big (2) _____ dog ran to us. He wanted to play with a ball.

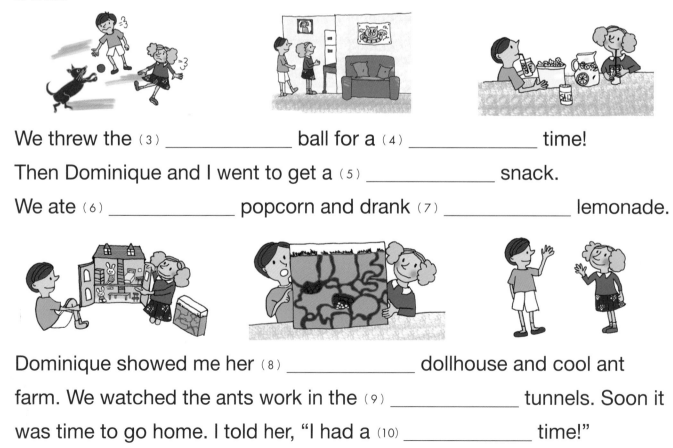

We threw the (3) _____ ball for a (4) _____ time!

Then Dominique and I went to get a (5) _____ snack.

We ate (6) _____ popcorn and drank (7) _____ lemonade.

Dominique showed me her (8) _____ dollhouse and cool ant farm. We watched the ants work in the (9) _____ tunnels. Soon it was time to go home. I told her, "I had a (10) _____ time!"

2 Complete the story with adverbs from the box. Then read the story aloud.

5 points each

early	happily	proudly	neatly	after
beautifully	later	outside	well	loudly

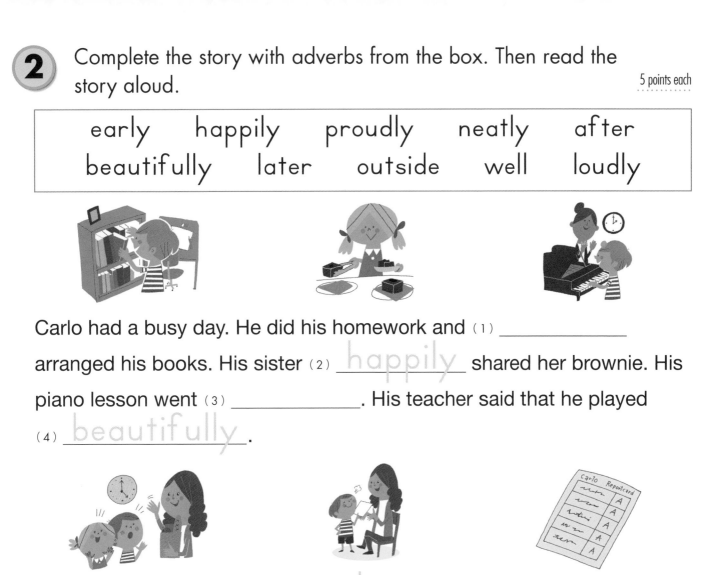

Carlo had a busy day. He did his homework and (1) _____

arranged his books. His sister (2) _happily_ shared her brownie. His

piano lesson went (3) _____. His teacher said that he played

(4) _beautifully_.

Carlo's mom came home (5) _early_ from work. He (6) _____

gave her his report card. Carlo got straight As! So his mom said, "We

should get ice cream (7) _____ dinner to celebrate!"

Carlo went (8) _____ to play with his sister before it got dark.

They made up songs and sang them (9) _____.

They went to get ice cream (10) _____ that

evening. Carlo hoped that he would have many more

days like this one.

Great story!

1 Complete each sentence with a subject or predicate from the boxes.

5 points each

Subjects	Predicates
My sister and I My mom His fluffy fur The vet	jumps wildly on our beds gave him some medicine was running feels better now

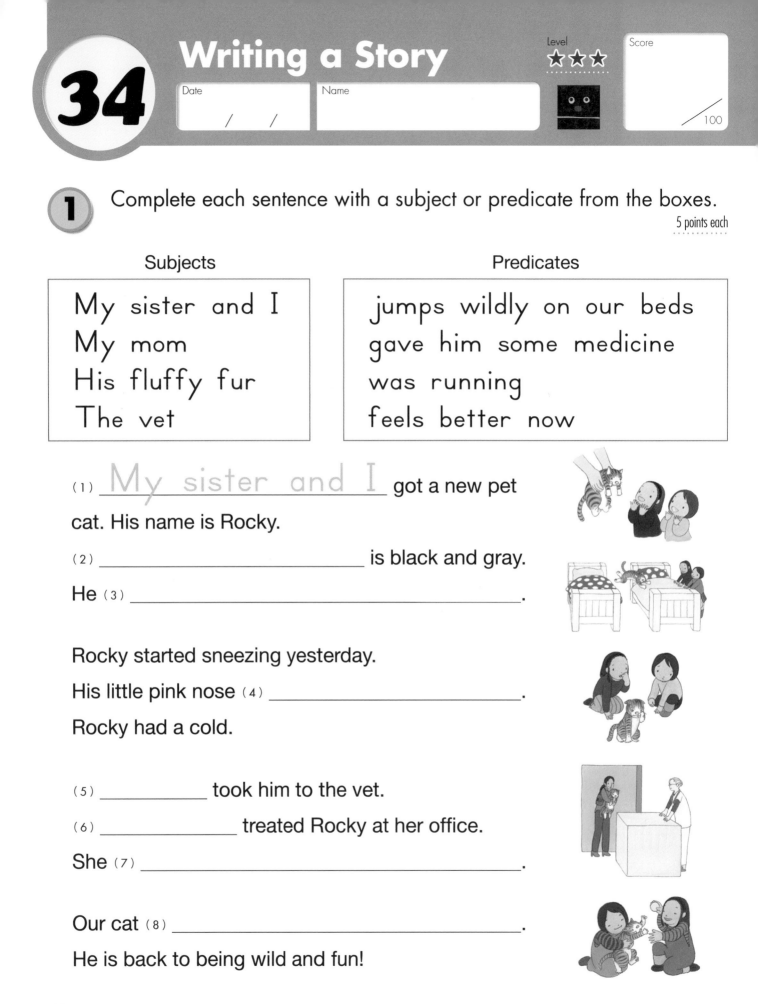

(1) _My sister and I_ got a new pet cat. His name is Rocky.

(2) _____ is black and gray.

He (3) _____.

Rocky started sneezing yesterday.

His little pink nose (4) _____.

Rocky had a cold.

(5) _____ took him to the vet.

(6) _____ treated Rocky at her office.

She (7) _____.

Our cat (8) _____.

He is back to being wild and fun!

2 Write the story with subjects and predicates from the boxes.   10 points each

Subjects	Predicates
The blue team	passed out drinks.
The second grade classes	was so much fun.
The teachers	won the sack race easily.
Field Day	won the tug of war fairly.
The red team	cheered loudly for each team.
The students	had a Field Day today.

(1) The second grade classes had a Field Day today.

(2) _____

(3) _____

(4) _____

(5) _____

(6) _____

Very clever!

Review

35

Level ☆☆

Score
/100

Date / /

Name

Complete each sentence with the plural form of the noun in the brackets.

5 points each

(1) The boy dropped some ⬜⬜⬜⬜⬜ .
[penny]

(2) My dad mashed the ⬜⬜⬜⬜⬜⬜ .
[potato]

(3) The playground was full of ⬜⬜⬜⬜⬜ .
[child]

(4) Every winter, the ⬜⬜⬜⬜ fly south.
[goose]

(5) I helped my neighbor rake up the ⬜⬜⬜⬜ .
[leaf]

2 Complete each sentence with a verb from the brackets.

5 points each

(1) People _____ when they are cold.
[shiver / shivers / shivered]

(2) We _____ for our team yesterday.
[cheer / cheers / cheered]

(3) Can you _____ this nail?
[hammer / hammers / hammered]

(4) Last year, she _____ in the school chorus.
[perform / performs / performed]

(5) The plane _____ the passengers and arrived on time.   [transport / transports / transported]

70   © Kumon Publishing Co., Ltd.

3 Complete each sentence with the past tense of the verb.

5 points each

(1) I read that book for my book report.

I _____ that book for my book report last year.

(2) She eats a sandwich at the picnic today.

She _____ a sandwich at the picnic yesterday.

(3) Gabriela buys a new pencil case.

Gabriela _____ a new pencil case last week.

(4) There is a boat at the dock now.

There _____ a boat at the dock, but it sailed away.

(5) Dennis has the flu this week.

Dennis _____ the flu all last week.

(6) We drive across the country in my family's van.

We _____ across the country last summer.

(7) He begins to write a letter.

He _____ to write a letter but had to stop for dinner.

4 Read the contraction. Then write the two words that each contraction represents.

3 points each

(1) wasn't   = _____ + _____

(2) it's   = _____ + _____

(3) she's   = _____ + _____

(4) couldn't = _____ + _____

(5) we're   = _____ + _____

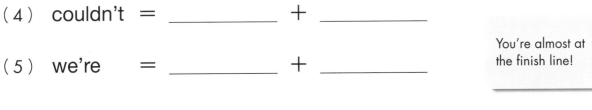

You're almost at the finish line!

1 Write each sentence with a subject and predicate from the boxes.

5 points each

Subjects	Predicates
A huge hawk My scraped knee The stormy sea Mom's gold ring	was very rough. is feeling better. flew up to its nest. fell into the sink.

(1) _____   _____
     Subject   Predicate

(2) _____   _____
     Subject   Predicate

(3) _____   _____
     Subject   Predicate

(4) _____   _____
     Subject   Predicate

2 Complete each sentence with an adverb from the brackets.

4 points each

(1) We must read _____.   [quietly / loudly]

(2) My sister jumped _____.   [under / over]

(3) Dad watched me _____.   [closely / slowly]

(4) We talked _____.   [wildly / softly]

(5) I walked _____.   [tiredly / excitedly]

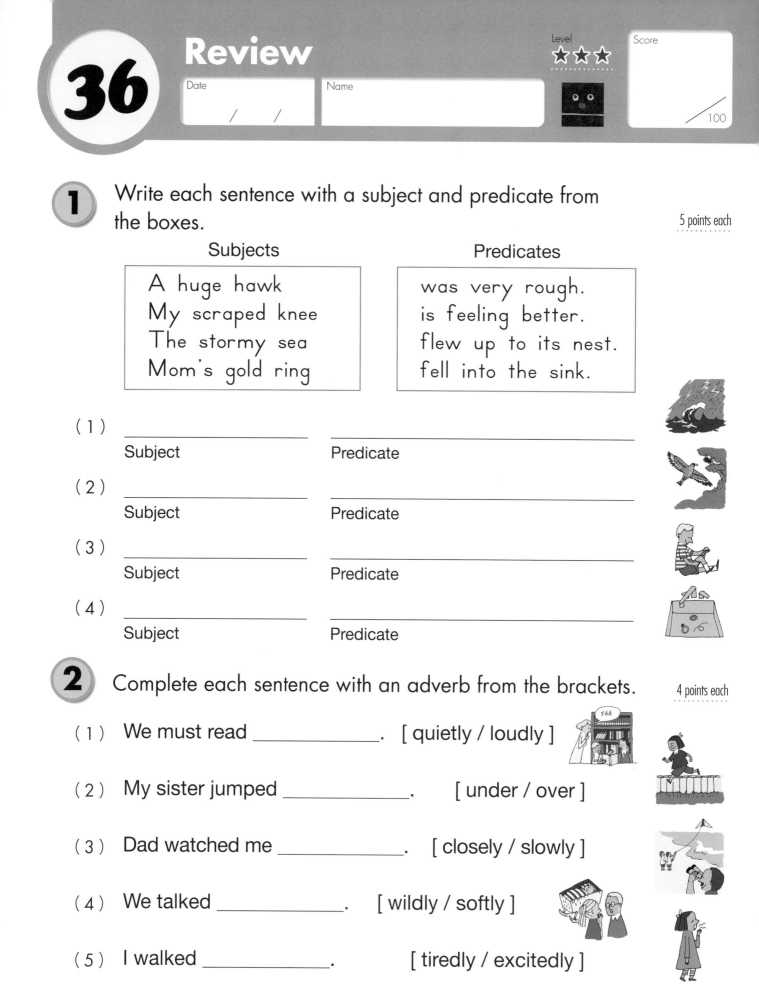

3 Complete each sentence with a verb and adverb from the boxes.

4 points each

Verbs

| cooked | ate | wore |
| shivered | is | |

Adverbs

daily   underground   outside
greedily   proudly

(1) Tama's aunt _____ breakfast _____.

(2) Our kitten _____ the treat _____.

(3) The treasure chest _____ _____.

(4) I _____ _____ in the snow.

(5) She _____ her gold medal _____.

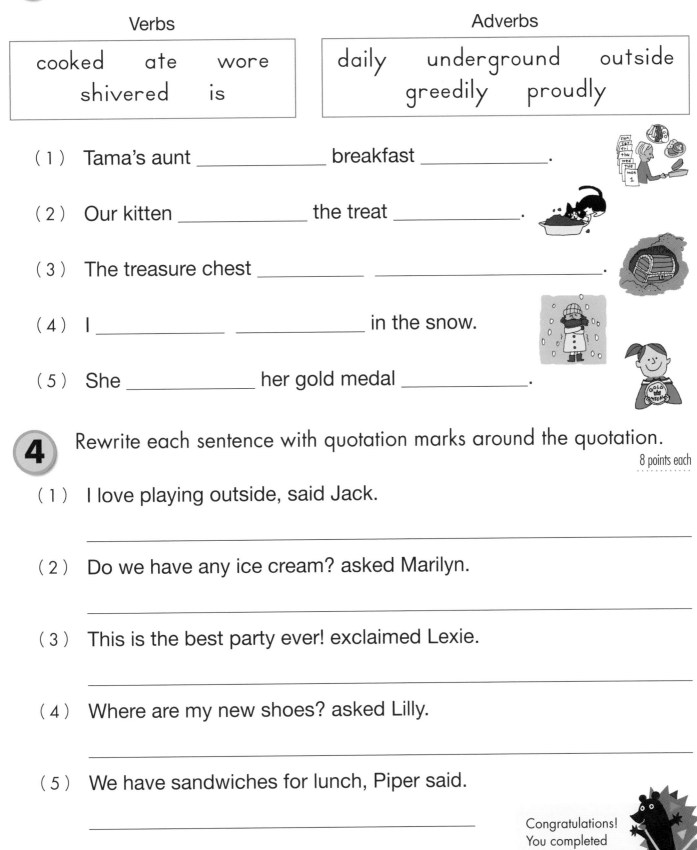

4 Rewrite each sentence with quotation marks around the quotation.

8 points each

(1) I love playing outside, said Jack.

_____

(2) Do we have any ice cream? asked Marilyn.

_____

(3) This is the best party ever! exclaimed Lexie.

_____

(4) Where are my new shoes? asked Lilly.

_____

(5) We have sandwiches for lunch, Piper said.

_____

Congratulations!
You completed
Grade 2 Writing!

_____

1 Vocabulary: Review
pp 2,3

1 (1) dinner (2) class (3) dress
(4) rabbit (5) strawberry
(6) spill (7) grass (8) apple

2 (1) dress (2) spill (3) rabbit
(4) strawberry

3 (1) dinner (2) class (3) strawberry
(4) grass (5) apple

4 (1) dinner (2) dress (3) class
(4) rabbit (5) grass (6) spill

2 Long Vowel Sounds: Review
pp 4,5

1 (1) bay / © (2) train / ⓑ (3) sea / ⓕ
(4) sheep / ⓓ (5) hike / ⓗ (6) slide / ⓐ
(7) rope / ⓘ (8) bone / ⓙ (9) blue / ⓖ
(10) flute / ⓔ

2 (1) blue (2) train (3) bay
(4) sea (5) hike (6) sheep
(7) slide (8) bone

3 (1) flute (2) rope (3) slide
(4) bone (5) sleep (6) phone

3 Vocabulary
pp 6,7

1 (1) joy (2) cowboy (3) coin
(4) noise (5) march (6) ache
(7) watch (8) catch

2 (1) joy (2) noise (3) march
(4) watch

3 (1) destroy / cowboy (2) point / coin
(3) chicken / march (4) scratch / catch
(5) anchor / ache

4 (1) scratch (2) march (3) point
(4) anchor (5) chicken (6) destroy

4 Vocabulary
pp 8,9

1 (1) cage (2) orange (3) badge
(4) bridge (5) mansion (6) television
(7) addition (8) invitation

2 (1) mansion (2) orange (3) addition
(4) badge

3 (1) huge / cage
(2) question / invitation
(3) vision / mansion
(4) ridge / bridge
(5) election / addition

4 (1) ridge (2) election (3) question
(4) vision

5 Pronouns: Review
pp 10,11

1 (1) He / She (2) I / You / you / me
(3) We / them (4) It
(5) They (6) him / her

2 (1) them (2) her (3) it (4) They

3 (1) He (2) it (3) We (4) They
(5) She (6) I (7) him (8) I
(9) her (10) you

6 Pronouns
pp 12,13

1 (1) this (2) That (3) us (4) This
(5) us

2 (1) this (2) that (3) us (4) that

3 (1) my / my (2) mine / my
(3) your / mine / your (4) yours / your

4 (1) your (2) my (3) your / this
(4) mine (5) mine (6) yours

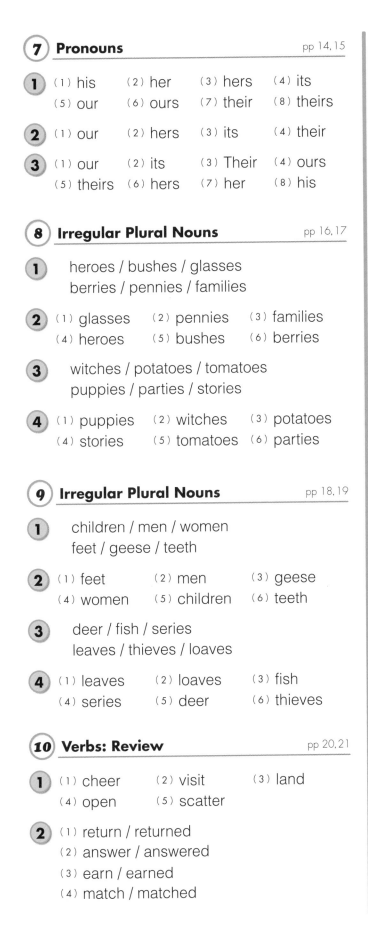

7　Pronouns　pp 14,15

1　(1) his　(2) her　(3) hers　(4) its
　　(5) our　(6) ours　(7) their　(8) theirs

2　(1) our　(2) hers　(3) its　(4) their

3　(1) our　(2) its　(3) Their　(4) ours
　　(5) theirs　(6) hers　(7) her　(8) his

8　Irregular Plural Nouns　pp 16,17

1　heroes / bushes / glasses
　　berries / pennies / families

2　(1) glasses　(2) pennies　(3) families
　　(4) heroes　(5) bushes　(6) berries

3　witches / potatoes / tomatoes
　　puppies / parties / stories

4　(1) puppies　(2) witches　(3) potatoes
　　(4) stories　(5) tomatoes　(6) parties

9　Irregular Plural Nouns　pp 18,19

1　children / men / women
　　feet / geese / teeth

2　(1) feet　(2) men　(3) geese
　　(4) women　(5) children　(6) teeth

3　deer / fish / series
　　leaves / thieves / loaves

4　(1) leaves　(2) loaves　(3) fish
　　(4) series　(5) deer　(6) thieves

10　Verbs: Review　pp 20,21

1　(1) cheer　(2) visit　(3) land
　　(4) open　(5) scatter

2　(1) return / returned
　　(2) answer / answered
　　(3) earn / earned
　　(4) match / matched

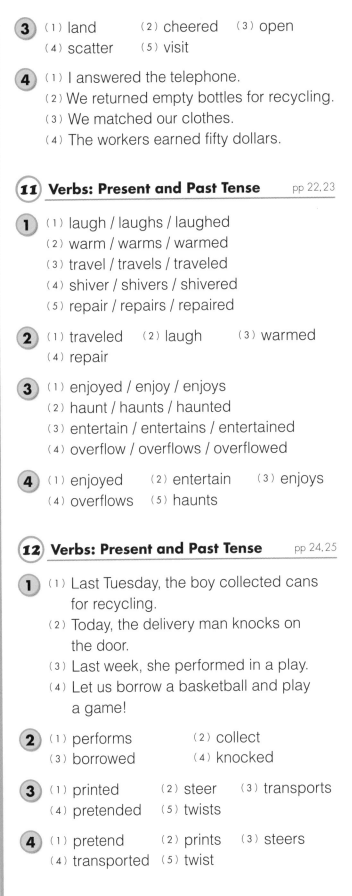

3　(1) land　(2) cheered　(3) open
　　(4) scatter　(5) visit

4　(1) I answered the telephone.
　　(2) We returned empty bottles for recycling.
　　(3) We matched our clothes.
　　(4) The workers earned fifty dollars.

11　Verbs: Present and Past Tense　pp 22,23

1　(1) laugh / laughs / laughed
　　(2) warm / warms / warmed
　　(3) travel / travels / traveled
　　(4) shiver / shivers / shivered
　　(5) repair / repairs / repaired

2　(1) traveled　(2) laugh　(3) warmed
　　(4) repair

3　(1) enjoyed / enjoy / enjoys
　　(2) haunt / haunts / haunted
　　(3) entertain / entertains / entertained
　　(4) overflow / overflows / overflowed

4　(1) enjoyed　(2) entertain　(3) enjoys
　　(4) overflows　(5) haunts

12　Verbs: Present and Past Tense　pp 24,25

1　(1) Last Tuesday, the boy collected cans
　　　for recycling.
　　(2) Today, the delivery man knocks on
　　　the door.
　　(3) Last week, she performed in a play.
　　(4) Let us borrow a basketball and play
　　　a game!

2　(1) performs　(2) collect
　　(3) borrowed　(4) knocked

3　(1) printed　(2) steer　(3) transports
　　(4) pretended　(5) twists

4　(1) pretend　(2) prints　(3) steers
　　(4) transported　(5) twist

(13) Plural Verbs: Review
pp 26, 27

1 (1) arrive (2) freeze (3) offer
(4) connect (5) listen

2 (1) The clown arrives at the party.
(2) The clowns arrive at the party.
(3) The child connects the puzzle pieces.
(4) The children connect the puzzle pieces.

3 (1) pastes (2) leave (3) toast
(4) scribble (5) combs

4 (1) scribble (2) leave (3) toast
(4) comb (5) paste

(14) Plural Verbs
pp 28, 29

1 We are / You are
They are / They are / They are

2 (1) are (2) are (3) is (4) are
(5) is (6) am (7) are

3 We have / You have / They have /
They have / They have

4 (1) have (2) have (3) has (4) has
(5) have (6) has (7) have

(15) Irregular Verbs
pp 30, 31

1 (1) carried / carry (2) hurried / hurry
(3) buried / bury (4) worried / worry

2 (1) hurried (2) buried (3) worried
(4) carried

3 (1) spy / spied (2) try / tried
(3) reply / replied (4) marry / married
(5) supply / supplied

4 (1) tried (2) replied (3) spied
(4) married (5) supplied

(16) Irregular Verbs
pp 32, 33

1 brought / thought / bought /
taught / caught

2 (1) taught (2) thought (3) brought
(4) caught (5) bought

3 rode / drove / wrote / broke / froze

4 (1) wrote (2) broke (3) froze
(4) drove (5) rode

(17) Irregular Verbs
pp 34, 35

1 (1) cut / cut (2) fit / fit (3) beat / beat
(4) read / read (5) set / set

2 (1) cut (2) beat (3) set
(4) read (5) fit

3 (1) began / begin (2) drank / drink
(3) rang / rings (4) swam / swim
(5) sang / sings

4 (1) swam (2) began (3) rang
(4) drank

(18) Irregular Verbs
pp 36, 37

1 ate / saw / went / led / left
was / was / were / did / had

2 (1) went (2) led (3) ate (4) left
(5) saw

3 (1) had (2) was (3) was (4) were
(5) did

4 (1) am (2) was (3) were (4) do
(5) had

19 Contractions — pp 38,39

1 (1) can't　(2) couldn't　(3) isn't
(4) wasn't　(5) don't　(6) didn't

2 (1) was / not　(2) do / not　(3) is / not
(4) can / not　(5) could / not　(6) did / not

3 (1) couldn't　(2) didn't　(3) isn't
(4) didn't　(5) can't

4 (1) didn't　(2) wasn't　(3) couldn't
(4) can't　(5) don't

20 Contractions — pp 40,41

1 (1) I'm　(2) We're　(3) It's
(4) He's　(5) She's

2 (1) he / is　(2) it / is　(3) she / is
(4) I / am　(5) we / are

3 (1) We're　(2) It's　(3) I'm
(4) She's　(5) He's

4 (1) I'm　(2) He's　(3) We're
(4) She's　(5) It's

21 Adjectives — pp 42,43

1 (1) juicy　(2) busy　(3) straight
(4) strong

2 (1) curvy　(2) weak　(3) calm
(4) dry

3 quick / quicker / quickest / longer
bright / brightest / small / smaller

4 (1) brighter　(2) smaller　(3) quicker
(4) longer

5 (1) brightest　(2) longest　(3) smallest

22 Subject and Predicate: Review — pp 44,45

1 (1) The boys　(2) A bear　(3) My dog
(4) Our cat　(5) Mom

2 (1) Her car needs new tires.
(2) The cat chased a mouse.
(3) Cara read two books yesterday.
(4) My friends are coming over.

3 (1) Three girls　(2) The lion
(3) Two giraffes　(4) The zookeeper
(5) The girls

4 (1) My goldfish / swims all day
(2) A dog / digs a hole
(3) My grandma / lives next door
(4) Tom / is a good friend

23 Longer Subjects — pp 46,47

1 (1) The little black dog jumped into the car.
(2) Grandpa's old car won a prize.
(3) An icy wind blew off my hat.
(4) My kind friend shared his sandwich.
(5) My big brother plays baseball.
(6) The hot apple pie cooled on the table.
(7) Mae's fancy dishes were on the table.
(8) Her helpful students cleaned the classroom.

2 (1) The little mouse　(2) A red rose
(3) Her curly hair　(4) The wet towels

3 (1) Min and Tara / did their homework
(2) The cold drink / tasted good
(3) The heavy book / fell off the shelf
(4) Jamie's dad / is cooking dinner

24 Longer Subjects — pp 48,49

1 (1) red　(2) tired　(3) blue　(4) little

2 (1) funny　(2) green　(3) soft
(4) tall　(5) messy

3 (1) The white snow covered the ground
   (2) The excited children went to the zoo
   (3) Jack's fast cars roll everywhere
   (4) The famous singer sang on stage
   (5) A tiny girl hid under the table
   (6) Two cute kittens played in the pet shop
   (7) Mom's beautiful coat got dirty
   (8) The lucky winner got a prize

25 Adverbs
pp 50,51

1 (1) quickly (2) badly (3) neatly
   (4) slowly

2 (1) noisily (2) messily (3) hungrily
   (4) happily

3 (1) quickly (2) gently (3) beautifully
   (4) hungrily (5) bravely (6) angrily
   (7) brightly (8) messily (9) loudly
   (10) quietly

26 Adverbs
pp 52,53

1 (1) happily (2) skillfully (3) tomorrow
   (4) outside

2 (1) first (2) up (3) around
   (4) after

3 (1) later (2) under (3) behind
   (4) over (5) earlier

4 (1) after (2) quickly (3) behind
   (4) sweetly

27 Longer Predicates
pp 54,55

1 (1) loudly (2) roughly (3) near
   (4) before

2 (1) will come over later
   (2) sings nicely
   (3) greeted us warmly
   (4) lost her ring often
   (5) climbed carefully

3 (1) exercises daily
   (2) happily live at the zoo
   (3) will go to school next week
   (4) told us to eat healthfully
   (5) has an elevator inside

4 (1) visit / today   (2) worked / quietly
   (3) ride / over   (4) wait / downstairs

28 Longer Predicates
pp 56,57

1 (1) My new classmates greeted me warmly.
   (2) His old sweatshirt fit tightly.
   (3) Arjun is next in line.
   (4) The soccer players played too roughly.

2 (1) will finally ski down
   (2) had a scratch
   (3) gobbled his food hungrily
   (4) live in burrows underground
   (5) closed the jar tightly

3 (1) sat safely on a high shelf
   (2) swung on the monkey bars
   (3) went to school cheerfully
   (4) was very lively

4 (1) My science projects are up on the wall
   (2) Lucia's gerbil ran under her dresser
   (3) Our neighbors politely waved at us
   (4) The snowman quickly melted in the sun
   (5) The beautiful painting was carried carefully

29 Review: Longer Subjects and Predicates pp 58,59

1
(1) stuck to the pan
(2) took the money greedily
(3) smiled sweetly
(4) pulled the wagon slowly
(5) hid the present upstairs
(6) munched on the grass quietly
(7) is on the bench
(8) drank the milk quickly

2
(1) (A happy little girl) / digs in the sand
(2) (The huge airplane) / took off quickly
(3) (The family) / comes here for a party
(4) (Our art class) / worked together nicely
(5) (The town's new playground) / was very crowded
(6) (Jacob) / washed the dirty clothes
(7) (The children's museum) / opens early
(8) (Brenden's little yellow backpack) / was in the car
(9) (The teammates) / listened to their coach patiently
(10) (The talented singer) / won many awards

30 Punctuation: Review pp 60,61

1
(1) The bird ate the juicy worm.
(2) We have a picnic with our teacher.
(3) My cat jumped swiftly onto the table.
(4) The cute baby laughed at us.
(5) The party starts at three o'clock.

2
(1) Mark / three dogs / ?
(2) the colored pencils / ?
(3) Sue / all her science homework / ?
(4) the birds / sweetly in the trees / ?
(5) we / to the beach this summer / ?

3
(1) Our school picnic is today.
(2) We will play games and eat outside.
(3) We will run relay races.
(4) Watch out for the runners! / Watch out for the runners.
(5) Which class won the race?
(6) What will we have for lunch?

31 Punctuation: Quotation Marks pp 62,63

1
(1) "Good morning, Mom,"
(2) "Can I have some more cookies?"
(3) "It is going to be a nice day today,"
(4) "Let's go swimming!"

2
(1) " "   (2) " "   (3) " "
(4) " "   (5) " "

3
(1) Here is your birthday present
(2) Chocolate chip is my favorite ice cream
(3) Are we going to miss practice
(4) We had a wonderful time

4
(1) "Gia went back to sleep,"
(2) "How old are you?"
(3) "We are so happy to see you!"
(4) "We will get popsicles today,"
(5) "Please come over to play,"

32 Writing Sentences: Review pp 64,65

1
(1) Our favorite park closed yesterday.
(2) Catch the vase! / Catch the vase.
(3) Can we go home?
(4) The tiny dog barked angrily.

2
(1) brightly   (2) loudly   (3) excited
(4) carefully   (5) wisely

3
(1) The hot soup spilled everywhere.
(2) The tiny fairy flew around merrily.
(3) Hiroshi sang the song loudly.
(4) Mrs. Bing fixed the swing outside.
(5) A brown coyote crept in the bushes.
(6) Saya and Josh stretch after class.

33 Writing a Story
pp 66,67

1 (1) sunny　(2) black　(3) red
(4) long　(5) tasty　(6) salty
(7) cold　(8) pretty　(9) tiny
(10) great

2 (1) neatly　　　　(2) happily
(3) well　　　　　(4) beautifully
(5) early　　　　　(6) proudly
(7) after　　　　　(8) outside
(9) loudly　　　　(10) later

34 Writing a Story
pp 68,69

1 (1) My sister and I
(2) His fluffy fur
(3) jumps wildly on our beds
(4) was running
(5) My mom
(6) The vet
(7) gave him some medicine
(8) feels better now

2 (1) The second grade classes had a Field Day today.
(2) The red team won the sack race easily.
(3) The blue team won the tug of war fairly.
(4) The students cheered loudly for each team.
(5) The teachers passed out drinks.
(6) Field Day was so much fun.

35 Review
pp 70,71

1 (1) pennies　　　(2) potatoes
(3) children　　　(4) geese
(5) leaves

2 (1) shiver　　　　(2) cheered
(3) hammer　　　(4) performed
(5) transported

3 (1) read　　　　　(2) ate
(3) bought　　　(4) was
(5) had　　　　　(6) drove
(7) began

4 (1) was / not　　　(2) it / is
(3) she / is　　　(4) could / not
(5) we / are

36 Review
pp 72,73

1 (1) The stormy sea / was very rough.
(2) A huge hawk / flew up to its nest.
(3) My scraped knee / is feeling better.
(4) Mom's gold ring / fell into the sink.

2 (1) quietly　(2) over　(3) closely
(4) softly　(5) tiredly

3 (1) cooked / daily
(2) ate / greedily
(3) is / underground
(4) shivered / outside
(5) wore / proudly

4 (1) "I love playing outside," said Jack.
(2) "Do we have any ice cream?" asked Marilyn.
(3) "This is the best party ever!" exclaimed Lexie.
(4) "Where are my new shoes?" asked Lilly.
(5) "We have sandwiches for lunch," Piper said.